# THE JEWS
# HEROES OF ETERNITY

*The Pivotal Role That God's Chosen People Have Played Throughout History ... And In The Coming End Times.*

by

Tommy **Lilja**

TULSA, OKLAHOMA

*Scripture quotations are from the New King James Version unless otherwise specified.*

THE JEWS — HEROES OF ETERNITY

© 2015 by Tommy Lilja

All rights reserved. Except as permitted under the U.S. Copyright Act of 1976, no part of this publication may be reproduced, distributed, or transmitted in any form or by any means, or stored in a database or retrieval system, without the prior written permission of the publisher.

TULSA, OKLAHOMA

*Published by:*
Emerge Publishing, LLC
9521B Riverside Parkway, Suite 243
Tulsa, Oklahoma 74137
Phone: 888.407.4447
www.EmergePublishing.com

Library of Congress Cataloging-in-Publication Data
Lilja, Tommy
The Jews — Heroes Of Eternity

ISBN: 978-0-9907694-7-7 Paperback

*Cover Design:* Christian Ophus | Emerge Publishing, LLC
*Interior Design:* Anita Stumbo
*Original Swedish Title:* Judarna — evighetens hjältar
*Translation:* Katie Lorentzon

Printed in the United States of America.

# CONTENTS

**Introduction · 5**

**PART I — God And The Jews Throughout History**
1. Jerusalem — A Cup Of Drunkenness To All The Surrounding Peoples · 9
2. The Jews — The Recurring Theme Throughout The Epochs Of History · 13
3. God And The Jews Throughout History · 19

**PART II — The People, The Land, The City And The Task**
4. The Covenant With Abraham · 29
5. The Jews — God's Chosen People · 37
6. If Anyone Has Ever Been A Jew, It's Jesus · 45
7. Israel, The Land Of Promise · 57
8. The People, The Land, The City And The Task · 65

**PART III — The Anti-Semitic History Of The Church**
9. "All Of The Victims Were Jews, All Of The Murderers Christians" · 77

**PART IV — The End Times**
10. Scattered To The Ends The Earth · 97
11. The Return — From The Four Corners Of The Earth · 103
12. Before The Final Battle: The Gospel Will Be Preached And The Jews Will Return Home · 115
13. The Final Battle · 123

**Epilogue · 133**

# INTRODUCTION

## by Tommy Lilja

THE JEWISH PEOPLE, the land of Israel and the city of Jerusalem have fascinated people for thousands of years. When I visited Israel for the first time several years ago, I too experienced a sense of the drawing power of the land and of the city. It was during this trip that a Bible passage from the prophetic book of Isaiah—verses that were previously unknown to me—suddenly came to life and I saw the Jewish people in their historical context.

After this experience much of the direction of my calling as a pastor and church builder changed. The result of this was that my church and I started Operation Great Exodus, an organization whose goal is to help Jews immigrate to Israel. Within the framework for this organization a teaching has been developed that clarifies the Jewish people's task in the history of God reaching out to man with salvation.

In the secularized environment in which the church is now active, and with the conflict in the Middle East a constantly relevant issue, there is a great need for the clarification of Biblical contexts concerning the Jewish people, as well as a reminder of the anti-Semitic elements of our church history. By generating insight into the history of the Jewish people, and by explaining the unique divine calling they have from God and their unique task in the history of salvation, I believe and hope that you as the reader—whether a Christian or just someone who is curious—will gain a better understanding of and love for the Jewish people, as well as be able to put the conflict in the Middle East into its historical context. ✡

# PART 1

## God And The Jews Throughout History

## Jerusalem — A Cup Of Drunkenness To All The Surrounding Peoples

THERE IS A PLACE in the world that has, throughout all of history, been at the center of events. In ancient times this place occupied a central location, one that was important for the superpowers of the time to control since the dominating superpower, Egypt, and its pharaohs, was located at one end of the corridor. The seashore of the Eastern Mediterranean constituted the highway of that time, and it served as a junction between Africa, Asia and Europe. The plain of Harmageddon was a giant roundabout where three major parts of the world met.

During the historical period of antiquity this place was governed by Rome, who did what they could in order to destroy the spiritual devotion the people had to the God they worshipped, a God they jealously claimed was the one and only God. Everything ended in catastrophe for the inhabitants of this land. Hundreds of thousands of people died when Rome put a stop to an uprising in the year 70 A.D. Sixty years later the people revolted yet again. This time the city was leveled to the ground and the remaining people were forced

# PART I — GOD AND THE JEWS THROUGHOUT HISTORY

to flee. A Roman capital was built where the former capital had been located, all for the purpose of obliterating the magnetic appeal that the place seemed to have, and still has, on many people.

It was here that a teaching about the one and only one God unfolded during the course of several intense decades; a teaching about the equal worth of all people and about the God who gave himself, as a man, to condemn the sin of man in himself.

For several centuries it seemed that this land and its capital had completed the role that they were to play. But during the 1100s the focus of the world was once again on this city, land and people. For the first time, the strength of two of the coming great cultures was felt in this epoch, a time we refer to as the era of the Crusades. It was here—where Nebuchadnezzar's armies marched, where Pharaoh's soldiers went forth and where the legions of Rome built multi-lane roadways for going out to battle—that the Crusaders of the west confronted the new superpower called Islam. The fighting between them went on for two centuries and the resulting bloodbaths were of historical proportions.

After the Crusades the land went into hibernation for long periods of time. But the city still found itself at the center of things. In the middle of the 1800s the land was reawakened. Its people, who had been in the Diaspora for nearly two centuries, began to turn their eyes back to their former homeland once again. It was as though history slowed down to a stop, waiting for the people to return to the city and the land. From northern Africa and the heart of Russia, foundations began to be laid for a second immigration. A people who had lived separately from one another for thousands of years, in totally foreign cultures, were reunited in a miraculous way when they returned to the land. And in less than 100 years the land was transformed from a desert to an oasis.

## The nation is born

*"Shall a nation be born at once?"* The prophet's question in Isaiah 66:8 gained renewed power when the country that had not been a

country for two millennia was suddenly born on May 14, 1948. The birthing pains continued when the entire Arab world declared war on this vulnerable, newborn child. But now it seemed that nothing could stop what was predestined to take place. Their attackers were forced back in a miraculous way as the God they had always claimed was the one and only God seemed to intervene in the background as their invisible defender. It was a match like that of David against Goliath—and David won once again.

So the dream came true. The people returned from all of the countries of the earth. The world stood by amazed and watched it happen. In one day, the nation was born, and within decades—in 1967 it was fully established. But the price that the people have had to pay to defend and uphold their own unique role in history has been incredibly high. Two thousand years of pogroms, alienation, suffering and death culminated in an additional six million people being annihilated within the space of a few years in the 1940s. But today they are back, and the city, people and land are at the center of world events now more than ever.

That land is Israel, the city is Jerusalem and the people are the Jews. At first glance, Israel is an ancient site of settlement as well as a political hotspot because of its geographically strategic location. But if we dig a little deeper we will discover that the land, the city and the people are much more than that. Together they make up one unit, a unit whose mission in history affects all the peoples of the earth. This mission will place this people, city and land in the center of history until all of time dissolves into eternity.

When the prophet Zechariah (Zec. 12:2-3) prophesied in the 700s B.C. that *"Behold, I will make Jerusalem a cup of drunkenness to all the surrounding peoples ... I will make Jerusalem a very heavy stone for all peoples; all who heave it away will surely be cut in pieces, though all nations of the earth are gathered against it,"* he probably didn't know how right he would be! Since this prophecy was given, the nations of the earth have, on different occasions throughout history, gathered against Jerusalem.

But note especially the words *"I will make Jerusalem a cup of drunkenness to all the surrounding peoples."* What an amazingly accurate description! Jerusalem, Israel and the Jews have been like a brew that has been placed in a cup that has inebriated the superpowers for thousands of years—the rulers of Babylon, the emperors of Rome, the Crusaders of Europe, the Popes of the Vatican, the mullahs of Islam, Hitler, Communism—and today that cup is inebriating the nations of the earth, always an item on the agendas of the White House, European Union and the Kremlin. Everyone seems to be drinking from that cup, reeling from its intoxicating effects. What could possibly explain the effect that Israel, Jerusalem and the Jews have on all of the world and on all of history? In the chapters to come, the truths that so many cannot see about Israel, Jerusalem and the Jews will be revealed to you. There is no question that you will be affected by those truths, but whether this teaching blesses you or provokes you remains to be seen. All I know is that Israel never leaves anyone unaffected! ✡

## The Jews — The Recurring Theme Throughout The Epochs Of History

WHEN YOU AND I as humans try to comprehend that time is something without a beginning or an end, our intellects tend to protest. Why? Because our thoughts are simply not big enough! That's why most people would claim that there must be a beginning and an end to all things. And that's what I believe as well. I believe that the very reason our intellects cannot accept infinity is because the history of mankind has both a beginning and an end!

So what exactly is time, then? The Bible teaches us that God is *"... from everlasting to everlasting"* (Psalm 90:2). Time could be explained as what happens between these eternities and everlastings. In other words, first there is eternity, followed by the breaking forth of history. The course of history is measured in time, but history and time will come to an end, and everything will return to eternity once again. So why is it so hard to comprehend eternity? Simply because we are created to think and to act within history—within time. When a person dies we say that he has "left time"; that is, that he now belongs to eternity, a state of being where time has ceased!

God is eternal and he is from everlasting to everlasting. Between these two eternities is world history. The history of the world starts with creation. *"In the beginning God created the heavens and the earth"* (Gen. 1:1). When God created the heavens and the earth, time "began." The course of time and the events of time become our history. So, God's purpose with mankind will at some point reach its end goal, and everything will return once again to eternity. In that way we will have gone from eternity to eternity. But what is the meaning of life, if everything that exists now is just going to end up in eternity anyway? You could summarize the meaning of history by saying this: history is the path to where and how you as a person will spend that eternity.

**The different epochs of history**

The Biblical description of history has a specific, concrete beginning: the story of creation. It also has an end: the end times. Of course, history is more than a beginning and an end. It also contains something in between. In the Bible you can read about the great epochs that world history goes through and what they mean for mankind. There are many different ways to divide up our history. But to make it simple and easy for everyone to understand, you can look at it in the following way, by dividing our history into seven epochs:

1. ***The epoch of innocence—from creation to the fall into sin.*** The first epoch was the time of innocence and paradise, when man spent time with God face to face. This epoch came to an abrupt end when Adam and Eve sinned (see Gen. 1–3).

2. ***The epoch of conscience—from the fall into sin to the flood.*** Here humans were separated from God and were left to build a society where their own conscience set the limits for good and evil. But

the evil of man was great and the entire world at that time was obliterated by the flood, an enormous natural catastrophe that drowned everything alive except for Noah, his family and a boat filled with animals of all kinds (see Gen. 4–9).

3. ***The epoch of kingdoms—from the flood to Abraham.*** After the flood, man entered into a new era. From Noah's family the number of people grew quickly. It has been said that Nimrod laid the foundation for all of the kingdoms of the earth. But the kingdoms that man built were filled with evil. Whereas the former epoch appealed to man's conscience, this epoch appealed to what people can accomplish together. The Bible shows that nothing is impossible for people who have united and determined to do something together. But since what they did was filled with evil, God intervened again and confused their speech, so that no one person could understand what the other was saying. The consequence of this was that humans began to spread all across the entire earth (see Gen. 10–11).

4. ***The epoch of the promise—from Abraham to the covenant on Sinai.*** From what we can understand from the Bible, there was always someone who was born throughout these epochs who sought God and found God's approval. Adam had a son named Seth, who in his turn had a son named Enosh. Noah had a son named Shem, and this continued for a long period of time. About 4,000 years ago something happened that would affect all of us. God revealed himself to the Semite Abraham, who at that time lived in the city of Ur, located in present-day Iraq. The promises that God made to Abraham were enormous. God told him to leave Ur and move to a very special land. There, God would make him into a great nation, and in the descendants of Abraham all nations would be blessed. You could call this an epoch whose promises and events changed all of world history and laid the foundation for the culture we live in today. Here, for the first time,

God's plan for the salvation of man is revealed clearly, as well as the preparations involved in setting a people apart from all other peoples, a people who would become God's chosen people (see Genesis 12–Exodus 19).

5. *The epoch of the law—from Sinai to Calvary.* Abraham "left time" and his grandson Jacob and all of his sons with their families were forced to immigrate to Egypt during a major famine. In Egypt the people grew in number. There were more than 600,000 of them. After 400 years in Egypt the entire Jewish people emigrated from Egypt, led by one of the most brilliant leaders in the history of the world, Moses. Pursued by Pharaoh, they fled into the Sinai desert and eventually stopped at the mountain of Horeb, or Mount Sinai. It was here that something fantastic happened. The Jewish people collectively entered into a covenant with God about being his people, representing him on the earth and being a nation chosen above all other nations. The people then conquered the land of Israel, resulting in the birth of the nation of Israel. This was during the time of "deferment." Out in the world, the evil of man grew more and more, but the covenant that God made with Abraham contained a plan of salvation. When Jesus died on Calvary, the first portion of the task that Abraham and the Jewish people had was complete (see Exodus 19–Acts 1).

6. *The epoch of grace—from Calvary to Jesus' second coming.* This is where we are right now. Two thousand years ago on the day of Pentecost, a world-changing movement was birthed that has touched and will touch all the nations of the world. Now God's message of salvation is reaching all people groups, while the Jewish people are scattered in the Diaspora. But the Bible teaches that at the end of this epoch—when the gospel has been preached to all nations—the Jewish people will once again return to Israel. This epoch will have an extremely dramatic conclusion that is played out in and around Jerusalem (see Acts–Revelation 22).

7. **The epoch of the Messiah—from the coming of the Messiah to re-entry into eternity.** Much has been written about this epoch. But I will just briefly mention that both Jews and Christians are waiting for the day that the Messiah will be revealed. During this age, creation will be restored and everything will culminate when the purposes of history and of time are fulfilled and all things re-enter eternity.

## The recurring theme

The theme of this book and a new revelation for many people—maybe even for you—is that throughout these seven historical epochs, a recurring theme can be seen that binds together and partly explains all of world history. That recurring theme is the Jews. Of all that has happened and is happening around us today, much more than what most people will admit can in one way or another be attributed to the Jews. When God called and chose the Jews at Mount Sinai it was to become his *"special treasure above all people ... a kingdom of priests and a holy nation"* (Ex. 19:5-6). They would become a nation that set itself apart from all other nations, and this difference would be one of the signs that they definitely were the Lord's people.

And that is also what has happened. Even if many people want to conceal it or others want to explain it in some other way, the fact still remains that there is something about the Jews that distinguishes them from all other people. They have undoubtedly, without comparison, been the people who more than any other have affected world history the most. Here are some short but clear examples.

Jesus, who influenced our entire western society, was a Jew. The Bible was written by Jews. Islam associates itself with Abraham and in one way has its roots in and is influenced by Judaism. Communism was founded by Karl Marx, a Jew. An overwhelming portion of the world's foremost authors, composers and scientists throughout history have been Jews. Albert Einstein, a pioneer in modern physics, was a Jew. Bob Dylan, one of the main leaders of the protest movement in the 1960s, is a Jew. Gene Simmons, leader of the legendary rock group Kiss, is a Jew. Steven Spielberg, the great film director, is a Jew. Henry Kissinger, one of the USA's most renowned secretaries of state, is a Jew. All of world politics today is influenced by Jews, a people who live in a country barely the size of the state of New Jersey.

Whatever anyone says or claims, no one can deny the fact that the Jews are "a treasured possession out of all nations." Why? That is a fair question, and in the following chapters that question will be answered, since the divine calling of the Jews is closely associated with the mission they have been given.

Without going into that mission right now, we can at least agree that there is a recurring theme that runs through all of world history and its epochs. That theme is Jerusalem, Israel and a unique mission. To put it simply, that theme is: the Jews. ✡

# 3

## God And The Jews Throughout History

WHEN THE PROPHET ISAIAH wrote and asked *"who has believed our report?"* (Isaiah 53:1), he was mainly referring to the future and to two historical events: the history of Israel's restoration and Jesus' redemptive death on the cross. Sometimes events occur that are so unusual and surprising that we find it hard to believe that they are true when we hear about them. Who ever thought that the Soviet Union would collapse into independent national states? Who ever thought that Yugoslavia would be destroyed by civil war, and who would ever have dared to believe in a reunited Germany? When reality surpasses what we could have only hoped for, we are often taken by surprise. But there is an invisible hand that influences all things. In the beginning God created the heavens and the earth. He put it all into motion. But he has not, as some would claim, simply left us to our fate. Just the opposite is true: he has been very active throughout the history of man, and he still is!

**God exists within time**
About 600 years before Christ, the Babylonian empire expanded under the leadership of one of the greatest and most influential leaders in world history, King Nebuchadnezzar. His strategy for total domination included deporting entire groups of people. The Jews were one of the peoples that were conquered by King Nebuchadnezzar. Over the course of thirty years the entire nation of the Jews was deported to Babylon in what became known as the Babylonian captivity. One of the first to be deported was Daniel, an intelligent young man who quickly found his place in the new land and had a brilliant career as a part of Nebuchadnezzar's administration. There were many things that made Daniel stick out. One was his great integrity—he refused to betray his ideals, a characteristic that earned him respect in the new land. Another thing was that he was very bright, with a sense of organization and leadership which eventually placed him at the absolute top of the leaders and statesmen of the Babylonian empire. But above all he was a man of God and a prophet, possessing a spiritual intuition that never failed him.

The Babylonian captivity lasted about seventy years. It seems as though God had prepared Babylon for receiving the Jewish people through two smaller deportations, the first in 605 B.C., the one Daniel was a part of. By the time a larger portion of the people came after the destruction of Jerusalem in 586 B.C., Daniel was already one of the most influential statesmen in Babylon and could therefore aid his newly arrived countrymen in finding their place in the temporary homeland. What is remarkable and could even be considered contradictory in this entire tragic period in Jewish history is that God was always there in the background.

It was this seemingly contradictory action by the God of Israel that was the main problem the prophet Habakkuk had when he foresaw the destruction of Jerusalem and the Babylonian captivity.

He questioned how God could send such a pagan people as the Babylonians to punish the Jews for their disobedience towards him. The answer the prophet Habakkuk received (Habakkuk 2:4) was that *"the just shall live by his faith"*—faith that the God of Israel knows what he is doing. He had saved the Jewish people so many times before. Many times what we lack is faith in God and in his sovereignty. He never leaves us, and he never leaves the world. But we don't always understand what exactly is happening around us. For us as humans, it's impossible to have the perspective of God. We are all like Habakkuk now and then. But believe me, we can trust in God. That special trust, the kind that emanates from faith, was typical for Daniel. Whatever the circumstances, he trusted God.

So when Daniel raised his voice in Babylon and with prophetic accuracy praised God, he also provided us with confirmation that God is an active participant in the developing course of history:

*Blessed be the name of God forever and ever, for wisdom and might are His. And He changes the times and the seasons; He removes kings and raises up kings; He gives wisdom to the wise and knowledge to those who have understanding.* Daniel 2:20–21

It is God, Daniel asserted, who *"changes times and seasons."* It is he who steers the course of history. It is also he who *"removes and raises up"* kings. So there is not a government or a parliament in the world that is not a calculated part of God's plans and purposes.

One of the clearest examples of this was seen during the 1980s. At that time the world had two superpowers—the Soviet Union and the USA—and everyone thought that it would remain so in the foreseeable future. Surely no one could have imagined a unified Germany either. But suddenly the political reality changed. A new leader emerged on the political world scene—his name was Gorbachev. He rose quickly to the top of the communist Soviet Union and spoke of a new time of change, of the Russian *perestroika*. His politics caused waves among the entire Soviet central committee at the time. In a few years the Soviet Union dissolved. The political analysts didn't dare believe what they saw happening, the political experts pinched themselves and asked if this was really happening, and the world's political leaders called summit meeting after summit meeting. Some years later the Berlin Wall fell, East and West Germany were reunited and everything had changed.

What had happened? What were the reasons behind all of this? Daniel gives us part of the answer in his prophetic proclamation. God "changes times and seasons" and removes and raises up kings. The secretary general of the central committee, Mikhail Gorbachev, and the former chancellor of Germany, Helmut Kohl, were used as tools in God's hand when he shook the Soviet empire. The borders opened and the Jewish portion of the population was freed from Communist captivity.

The amazing parallel to the Babylonian captivity is revealed clearly in the light of what we now know: seventy years after the Babylonian captivity, the first Jews returned to Israel. Seventy years after the Bolshevik Revolution that closed the borders to the Russian Jews and basically made them prisoners within the Soviet state, the Soviet Union split. Less than ten years after that, a million Jews had left the former Soviet and, like their ancestors who had left Babylon after seventy years, they returned home to Israel, the Holy Land. Both then and now it was through the intervention of God that this took place. It was written by the prophet Isaiah that the Lord God, when the time had come, would *"say to the north, 'Give them up!' and to the south, 'Do not keep them back!' Bring my sons from afar and my daughters from the ends of the earth—everyone who is called by my name."* (Isaiah 43:6–7). And the countries of the north gave them up. One million Jews re-immigrated to Israel in the 1990s after a long, long journey.

The second effect of the collapse of the Soviet Union was that the area was opened again to the gospel. Tens of thousands of new churches have been started since then and millions of people have come to faith in God. Times and seasons have most certainly changed in that part of the world. On the surface there are likely many explanations, but for those who dig deeper it is easy to believe that it is God who has been at work all along. With great proficiency he is controlling world history, all so that his plans and purposes will be fulfilled.

## God's promises to the Jews exist within time

God's promises also have their place within time; his promises to the world as well as to Israel. We will study the promises more closely later, especially when we look at the land, the city, the people and their mission. But it is appropriate to briefly touch on God's promises here, those he has given to the Jewish people throughout the millennia.

The promises are important from several viewpoints, not only to confirm what God has given or will give to or do for Israel, but also to fight back against all of the lies out there concerning Israel. Two of the main attacks are anti-Semitism and the replacement theology. Unfortunately, the second one has been fabricated by the Church itself, and we have done all we can to keep the first lie alive. Replacement theology developed during the church's second and third centuries and was settled upon at the church meeting in Nice in the year 325. Of the many mistakes and violations made by the church, the decisions made here were probably the worst. The claim this theology makes is that the church has replaced the Jews as God's people. It claimed that the Jews were forever rejected by God. Some church leaders even felt that it would be just as good to kill all of them at once, since they were already condemned to eternal annihilation both in this life and in the afterworld. This false teaching would prove to be, as we will see later in the chapter about the history of anti-Semitism, the starting point of one of world history's most comprehensive persecutions of a people, culminating in the Holocaust during World War II.

The replacement concept was a theological blunder that cut off the very life of the church, since the New Testament obviously teaches that Israel is the true olive tree, the root itself, and that the church is the wild olive shoot that has been grafted in (see Romans 11:16–19). And unfortunately it has also been the case throughout history that the institutionalized church has always persecuted two groups: the Jews and the revival Christians. Revival Christians are the part of the church that has continually—with the power of the gospel, not military power—taken the gospel to new places. It is also revival Christianity that has defended the Jews, but this movement has not been able to make itself heard until the last 300 years, first in the USA and later in Europe, for the simple reason that independent churches were previously forbidden by law.

It is hard to understand how this could have happened when the New Testament is so full of teaching that emphasizes the Jewish people's special place in God's heart. It is surprising that the church has been able to close its eyes to these obvious statements. Paul writes, in a quote that is often used by Christians, that all of God's promises have their "yes" and "amen" in Christ (see 2 Corinthians 1:20). Note carefully the word "all." So all of the promises must also mean the promises to the Jews. "But," someone may ask, "aren't all of God's promises to the Jews fulfilled?" Absolutely not. Certain promises are still awaiting their entire fulfillment! That is why everything that has to do with Israel is becoming so very interesting and is gaining such explosive power. Israel and the Jews are like God's prophetic clock.

**So what are the promises?**
God's promises to Israel can be divided into four groups: the promises to the people, the promises about the land, the promises about the city and the promises about the task. All of these promises have received their "yes" and "amen" in Christ. Some of these are fulfilled; others are waiting to be fulfilled. But for the church it is important to realize that those promises are confirmed in Christ. To further emphasize the significance of God's promises I want to point to God's recognition of Abraham and his descendants:

*By Myself I have sworn, says the LORD, because you have done this thing, and have not withheld your son, your only son—blessing I will bless you, and multiplying I will multiply your descendants as the stars of the heaven and as the sand which is on the seashore; and your descendants shall possess the gate of their enemies. In your seed all the nations of the earth shall be blessed, because you have obeyed My voice.* Genesis 22:16–18

In this proclamation, which was made after Abraham was ready to sacrifice the son of promise on Mt. Moriah, God swore by his own self that in Abraham's offspring all the nations of the world would one day be blessed. This one promise covers, contains and embraces everything: the people, the land, the city and the task—and, actually, even you and me. ✡

# PART II

## The People, The Land, The City And The Task

## The Covenant With Abraham

THROUGHOUT the course of history the Jewish people have never ceased to amaze. With their zeal they have aggravated those in power all over the world by refusing to let themselves be assimilated into the cultures of other countries. Although the Jews have successfully blended in as far as everyday life is concerned, they have still always remained different under the surface.

There are customs, traditions and rules that the core of the Jewish people have never forsaken, something that has forever held—and still holds—together the Jewish identity. Time after time, anti-Semitic actions have tested the loyalty of the Jews, but nothing has been able to "break" their faithfulness to their identity and to their roots.

One man in particular, Haman the Agagite, was a powerful man who has proven to be significant for many anti-Semitic leaders later on in history as well. Haman was the prime minister and in charge of the Persian kingdom during the reign of King Xerxes I6 in the 400s B.C. Haman the Agagite should actually never have even existed, since King Saul received an order to completely eliminate the

Amalekites, Haman's ancestors. But King Saul did not obey God's command, a selfish mistake that had far-reaching consequences when history would strike back hundreds of years later against the Jews. Haman, well aware of the history of his own ancestors, planned to now eliminate all of the Jews in the Persian kingdom. But thanks to Esther, one of the king's queens, Haman's plans failed when she put her life at stake and intervened on behalf of her people the Jews (see the book of Esther in the Old Testament).

What I want to point out in this dramatic story is the argument that Haman the Agagite used in his attitude against the Jewish people when he sought King Xerxes' approval for his plans. He said:

*There is a certain people scattered and dispersed among the people in all the provinces of your kingdom; their laws are different from all other people's, and they do not keep the king's laws. Therefore it is not fitting for the king to let them remain. If it pleases the king, let a decree be written that they be destroyed.* Esther 3:8–9

"There is a certain people different from all other people." In one sense this is a very accurate description of the Jews. But the question could be asked: wouldn't it be better to give up your Jewishness and let yourself be assimilated into new cultures and groups? Much suffering could have undoubtedly been avoided for millions of people throughout the millennia if that had been the case! Of course this claim makes sense, but it must be weighed against two other factors. The first is the Jewish people's historic mission, which is a recurring theme in the rest of this book. The other is their integrity.

I have many Jewish friends who are precious to me and whom I value highly. Sometimes when we are together I am provoked by their Jewish integrity and its rigidity, which can often lead to heated discussions. But it is truly amazing that they have such integrity—it is something that cannot be bought! What anti-Semitism hates the Jew for, I respect and love him for, since there is something in him that is invulnerable. This should set an example for us and serve as hope to all of us in a time when so many others so easily forsake their ideals and give up on their promises.

But how did the Jews become Jews? How did their identity emerge? It all started long ago in the city of Ur with a man named Abraham.

## God calls Abraham the Semite

> *Now the LORD had said to Abram: "Get out of your country, from your family and from your father's house, to a land that I will show you. I will make you a great nation; I will bless you and make your name great; and you shall be a blessing. I will bless those who bless you, and I will curse him who curses you; and in you all the families of the earth shall be blessed."* Genesis 12:1–3

The tower of Babel was built on the large plateau between the Tigris and the Euphrates rivers. According to the Bible, it was from this place that the Lord God spread out mankind across the entire world. It is here that the first traces of the world we live in today can be found.

This is also where Terah lived. He was a direct descendant of Shem, who was one of Noah's three sons. It was in the culture of this region, filled with pluralism and worship of a god who reappears throughout history, "the queen of heaven," that Terah's son Abraham grew up. One day Abram met God in a revelation. Very resolutely, God told Abram to leave his homeland and settle in a land that God would show him. God promised that in this land Abram's offspring would grow throughout the years and become a great nation, a very special people. Whoever blessed this people would receive God's blessing, but whoever cursed this people would come under a curse, a phenomenon I would say we have also seen throughout history.

For example, Beirut was a flourishing city until it opened up for anti-Semitic groups in the 1970s. Great Britain has still not escaped the economic depression that resulted when it changed its politics regarding Israel in the 1920s. When Swedish prime minister Olof Palme implemented policies unfavorable toward Israel, Sweden simultaneously fell into an economic depression that culminated in the beginning of the 1990s. The upswing for the Swedish economy came, interestingly enough, through another social democratic leader, Göran Persson. He broke with the traditional social democratic policies toward Israel when he invited the leaders of the world to an international conference addressing the Holocaust. The fruit of that conference was a book entitled Tell Ye Your Children, an essay about the Holocaust. Neither is it a coincidence that the country with the greatest economy in the world today, the USA, has always been a friend to Israel.

**The blood covenant**

> *When the sun went down and it was dark there appeared a smoking oven and a burning torch that passed between those pieces. On the same day the LORD made a covenant with Abram, saying: "To your descendants I have given this land."* Genesis 15:17–18

Many years after God's directive to Abram to leave the city of Ur he came as a seventy-five-year-old with his wife Sarah and his nephew Lot to the land we know today as Israel. Here the childless Abraham is promised a son and through dreams and visions, a strong conviction is birthed in Abraham that God is mighty to fulfill his promises.

One day Abraham senses again that God is speaking to him in a very special way. He is told to perform a rite where an animal is cut into two halves. What happens then contains a symbolism whose meaning has been lost in western culture, but is still understood by people in the third world. God, through this special rite, was going to enter into covenant with Abraham.

An interesting comparison can be found in the life of David Livingstone. The stories about him say that the most important reason for his survival and ability to cross into new territory in the deepest parts of Africa was that he had entered into so many blood covenants with different tribe leaders.

So what does a blood covenant signify? Since it is performed in almost exactly the same way in all cultures we know how it is done. An animal is sacrificed, often a bull. Sometimes both sides clothed themselves in one half of the animal, and they met inside the animal halves, and then mixed each other's blood from opened wounds somewhere on their bodies. But what caused the African tribes to respect Livingstone was not merely the many typical scars that testified to the many blood covenants he had made, but rather what the covenants stood for.

A blood covenant was the most demanding of the covenants. It meant that you took full responsibility for each other and each other's families. You became blood brothers. If something should happen to the one, it was the responsibility of the other to respond, to take care of the other's wife, to raise the other's children, etc. Harming David Livingstone therefore meant that you were also harming his blood brothers and thus accumulating many enemies.

When God tells Abraham to cut the animal in two, Abraham knows that something big is about to happen. He understands the symbolism. A covenant is going to be entered into, but he could probably never, in his wildest imagination, have believed that God would be one "blood brother" and he the other.

The symbolism is powerful here. Harming Abraham would be the same thing as going after God himself. But for me as a Christian there is even more depth to the covenant. One of the cornerstones of any covenant is "like for like." But what could Abraham give to God that could be compared with what God could do for Abraham? This is where the greatness of Abraham's personality shines through. Childless, he receives the promise that Sarah, through a miracle, will get pregnant, and she does at the age of ninety. A few years later God tells Abraham to—in an act that seems to be in complete contradiction to the covenant—go to Mt. Moriah to offer his son Isaac as a sacrifice to God. The Bible tells us that Isaac himself carries the wood for the sacrificial fire. When Abraham raises the knife in order to sacrifice Isaac, he is stopped by an angel of God—he has passed the test!

Two thousand years later God's son Jesus is on the way to Mt. Moriah, where the city of Jerusalem has been built. Like Isaac, he is an only son, born through a miracle. He also carries the wood himself—the cross—to the site of sacrifice, Calvary. When Jesus dies it is God's son who is sacrificed. "Like for like" is a requirement of the blood covenant. Abraham was ready to sacrifice Isaac for God, and now God sacrifices his own son Jesus for Abraham. A sacrifice that in the future will prove itself to be the salvation for us all, both Jews and Gentiles.

**The sign of the covenant**

> *I will establish a covenant with you and greatly increase you. You will be the father of many nations and kings will come from you. And my covenant with you will last from generation to generation; it will be an everlasting covenant. The whole land of Canaan I will give you and your descendants as an everlasting possession. And this is the covenant you are to keep: Every male among you shall be circumcised as a sign of the covenant between you and me. My covenant in your flesh is to be an everlasting covenant.* Genesis 17:1–14 (author's summary)

Many years had passed since God and Abraham entered into covenant with one another. Now God revealed himself to Abraham yet again. It was as though Abraham, now nearing the end of his life, had needed to mature even more before being able to receive the promises and the requirements that were revealed here regarding the covenant. He would be the father of nations. Nations and kings would come from him and even in the future, God would reveal himself to his descendants and the land would belong to Abraham's people forever. As an eternal sign that his descendants belonged to the covenant that God had made with Abraham, all of the men would be circumcised.

A lot can be said about circumcision; the act itself contains strong symbolism. Once the operation has been done it is impossible to reverse! Once the covenant was made it was an eternal covenant, impossible to reverse. It was a covenant that would take Abraham's descendants through many hardships. It was a covenant, it would turn out, that left no room for turning back. Whether the Jew wants to or not he is, because of the covenant, forever an active part of God's plans and purposes for the world. ✡

# 5

## The Jews — God's Chosen People

AFTER MANY YEARS in exile and lots of hard work, Jacob, Abraham's grandson, is finally on his way home to the promised land. He longs to see his father Isaac but dreads meeting up with his brother Esau. A long time has passed since he had to flee after betraying his brother. Now he is on the run again, this time from his uncle Laban. He has no choice but to face his brother and ask forgiveness. It is at this time that something remarkable happens to Jacob the night before he reaches the outermost borders of the land of Canaan: he meets God face to face! For some reason the encounter turns into a struggle, and Jacob fights with God in something that the Bible portrays as a wrestling match. Just before dawn God strikes Jacob on the hip, a blow that will cause him to limp for the rest of his life. God also gives him a new name, Israel, which means "wrestles with God" (see Genesis 32).

Israel, "Wrestles with God," is blessed with twelve sons. From these twelve men emerge the people that we know today as the Jews. All of Israel's descendants have some of Jacob's blood in them, and share in his characteristics. Jacob became Israel, he who wrestled with God, and through the millennia his descendants have in their own way "wrestled with God."

## From 70 starving nomads to 600,000 Israelites

Israel's (Jacob's) time in the promised land turned out to be tough. After many years of famine, the family that now numbered about seventy people was forced to migrate to Egypt, where it was rumored that grain was plentiful. They probably only intended to stay a short while in Egypt. But just as God had forewarned Abraham, their stay would end up lasting for 400 years.

> *Know certainly that your descendants will be strangers in a land that is not theirs, and will serve them, and they will afflict them four hundred years. Genesis 15:13*

In Egypt this little group of people grew quickly and after 400 years there were so many of them that they had become a threat to the entire empire of Pharaoh. It all culminated in a power struggle and test of strength between Pharaoh and the Jewish people, or as the Bible puts it, a struggle between God and the gods of Egypt. One of Egypt's former princes, the Jew Moses, stood at the forefront for the Jewish people. He challenged Pharaoh to let the Jewish people go so that "they can hold a feast for the Lord in the desert" (see Exodus 5:1). The power struggle became intense and ended in catastrophe for Pharaoh. He was forced to let the Jewish people go, and with the Egyptians' wealth in hand they marched through the Red Sea and the Sinai Desert. After a few months they came to Mt. Sinai, where they set up camp for nearly a year.

## God calls the nation of Israel

> *"Now therefore, if you will indeed obey My voice and keep My covenant, then you shall be a special treasure to Me above all*

*people; for all the earth is Mine. And you shall be to Me a kingdom of priests and a holy nation." These are the words which you shall speak to the children of Israel.* Exodus 19:5–6

At the foot of Mt. Sinai all of Israel was summoned to meet the God who once called their forefather Abraham to leave the city of Ur. God was going to reveal some of the purposes he has always had for his people. It must have been an awesome experience as Moses raised his voice for all to hear, and spoke of God's royal calling to a people who only months ago were slaves in Egypt. They were to become "his treasured possession, a kingdom of priests, a holy nation."

The call was to the entire nation, to Israel. God did not present this prospect of becoming his possession solely to Moses or to the leaders, but to all the people as a collective unit. The call was a choice, because if they answered, it would hold for all of Israel's descendants until the end of time (see 2 Samuel 7:23–24). The call was unbreakable. The Jews could leave God, but not the covenant!

**"We will do everything the Lord has said"**
"All that the LORD has spoken," all the people said with one voice, "we will do." It was a collective decision, with everyone answering God's calling. It says that: "Moses brought back the words of the people to the LORD" (see Ex. 19:8). "They say yes," Moses said to God. But the decision was a big one and would have far-reaching consequences for all of Israel's future children, so Moses had to return to the people and ask the same question once again. This time he read aloud, so that everyone could hear, what it would mean to be a people chosen above all other peoples, to be a holy nation of priests to the one and only God.

*Then he took the Book of the Covenant and read in the hearing of the people. And they said, "All that the LORD has said we will do, and be obedient." And Moses took the blood, sprinkled it on the people, and said, "This is the blood of the covenant which*

39

## PART II — THE PEOPLE, THE LAND, THE CITY AND THE TASK

*the LORD has made with you according to all these words."*
Exodus 24:7–8

The covenant that was agreed upon at the foot of Mt. Sinai would have far-reaching consequences for the people of Israel and the entire world. That was why it was important that the entire nation had a choice in the matter. God doesn't force anyone to do anything! His plan was for a great nation to come from Abraham's descendants. Out of this nation other nations, kings and salvation would come to the whole world. One of the basic principles of creation is free will. Abraham, Isaac and Israel (Jacob) answered the call from God, but for the sake of God's righteousness, the whole nation had to once again have the chance to choose to either answer or reject the call that Abraham received.

At Mt. Sinai there stood a mighty people so large in number and so powerful that they terrified Egypt and Pharaoh. Six hundred thousand men! Such a number must have meant that the people totaled several million. They were all lined up now before God whose Spirit rested on the mountain. So when the question was called out by Moses, the millions of people answered with one voice: "We will do everything the Lord has said; we will obey!", an answer that has echoed throughout history.

The covenant contained every directive and instruction that was needed. The covenant gave the people of Israel wealth, success, land, influence and blessing. But the covenant also meant that a curse would come over each and every person who broke the covenant. The wonderful thing about the covenant is to see how God has blessed this people. But it is also terrifying to see how the punishment that would come over the people if they broke that covenant has also been fulfilled, word for word, throughout the passages of history.

*If you diligently obey the voice of the LORD your God, to observe carefully all His commandments which I command you today, the LORD your God will set you high above all nations of the earth. And all these blessings shall come upon you and overtake you, because you obey the voice of the LORD your God … But if you do not obey the voice of the LORD your God, to observe carefully all His commandments and His statutes which I command you today, all these curses will come upon you and overtake you.* Deuteronomy 28:1–2, 15

A role model for many future civilizations Israel stayed at Mt. Sinai for nearly a year. It was here that God founded the nation of Israel that would become a role model for many of the world's coming kingdoms. When Israel left Egypt they had no army, no schools, no governors or mayors, and no judicial system. When they set up camp at Mt. Sinai Israel received, through a unique revelation, God's instructions for how an entire nation should be organized. God gave them the pattern for how to build a nation:

*Then the LORD said to Moses, "Come up to Me on the mountain and be there; and I will give you tablets of stone, and the law and commandments which I have written, that you may teach them … According to all that I show you, that is, the pattern of the tabernacle and the pattern of all its furnishings, just so you shall make it."* Exodus 24:12 & 25:9

The first task was to build a meeting place with God—the tabernacle. The people accepted this assignment with great devotion. Everyone wanted to get involved and help build. When Moses asked the people to send funds for the building of the tabernacle they gave so much that Moses had to ask them to stop bringing their gifts! After several months the work was finished and Moses inspected the work with great satisfaction:

*According to all that the LORD had commanded Moses, so the children of Israel did all the work. Then Moses looked over all the work, and indeed they had done it; as the LORD had commanded, just so they had done it. And Moses blessed them ... Then the cloud covered the tabernacle of meeting, and the glory of the LORD filled the tabernacle.* Exodus 39:42–43 & 40:34

The key word in all of their efforts was "blueprint," organizing the work according to the exact instructions that God gave Moses. In Leviticus we can read of how this revelation increased and God gave thorough instructions that included all areas of life.

- **Ethics and spiritual life:** In the Ten Commandments God provided some standards for their spiritual life and an appropriate set of morals.
- **Civil rights:** Laws that regulate relationships between citizens in a society.
- **Ceremonial rules:** Instructions on how to worship God.

After a year of preparations the newborn nation of Israel was ready to break camp at Mt. Sinai and possess the land that God had promised them. It must have been one of the largest camping sites the world has ever seen. According to some calculations the camp took up an area of about thirty square kilometers. In Numbers we can read about the final preparations that took place before breaking camp in the Sinai Desert. A careful population count was taken, the tribes were organized, the leaders' assignments were repeated, and additional leaders were appointed. Two signal trumpets were made, the importance of sanctification was emphasized again, and the last thing they did in the Sinai Desert was to celebrate the Passover, the festival of the slaughtered lamb. The covenant was renewed.

Now the Lord showed up and took the lead in a pillar of cloud. The silver trumpets signaled the procession to begin and in perfect order Israel broke camp. With the tribe of Judah in the lead, the newborn nation began its journey toward the promised land.

**Joshua takes possession of the land**
Moses, one of the greatest leaders in the history of the world, brought

the people through the desert up toward the promised land but was himself not the one who led the invasion and conquest. On the heights of Moab, present-day Jordan, he turned over his leadership to an adept young man named Joshua. Under Joshua's command, the land of Canaan was conquered and then divided into twelve portions. The people had established themselves in the land.

## An everlasting covenant

There is one question that has been asked continually since the breakthrough of Christianity and the destruction of Jerusalem in 70 A.D.: How long will the covenant between the Jews and God last (or when will it end)? How long can the Jews as a people make a claim on the covenant and the promises of the covenant? The answer has always been, and always will be, that based on the teaching of the Bible, the covenant is eternal.

> *Thus says the LORD, who gives the sun for a light by day, the ordinances of the moon and the stars for a light by night, who disturbs the sea, and its waves roar (the LORD of hosts is His name): "If those ordinances depart from before Me, says the LORD, then the seed of Israel shall also cease from being a nation before Me forever."* Jeremiah 31:35–36

Not until the sun stops shining, not until order in the heavens ceases, will the people of Israel cease to be the Lord's people above all other peoples. Note well that this is not a statement or an interpretation of God's will, but that it is God himself who says it. The prophet Samuel asserts the same truth when he exclaims in a powerful prayer to God:

> *And who is like Your people, like Israel, the one nation on the earth whom God went to redeem for Himself as a people, to make for Himself a name—and to do for Yourself great and awesome deeds for Your land—before Your people whom You redeemed*

*for Yourself from Egypt, the nations, and their gods? For You have made Your people Israel Your very own people forever; and You, LORD, have become their God.* 2 Samuel 7:23–24

**Summary and consequence**
There is only one nation that has ever entered into covenant with God, and that nation is the Jewish people. This covenant is eternal whether somebody, Jewish or Gentile, wants it to be or not!

The consequence for "all other nations" depends on what stance they take toward the Jewish people. The key element of the "blood covenant" that God made with Abraham is that the two sides stand up for one another. So many times the Jewish people, alone and outcast, have stood up for their covenant with the one and only God, and they have had to pay a high price for it.

In the same way God will always stand up for the people he has made an eternal covenant with. The nation or person who does good toward Israel does good toward God himself, and whoever curses Israel draws a curse upon himself: "I will bless those who bless you and I will curse him who curses you" (Gen. 12:3).

For the Jew this also has far-reaching consequences since he, through his forefathers, was at Mt. Sinai when the covenant went into effect. It was not an individual covenant but a collective covenant. It didn't apply to the individual but to the people. The contents and consequences of the covenant—both blessings and curses—are therefore at work in and through the Jew until eternity, whether he wants them to be or not. ✡

# 6

## If Anyone Has Ever Been A Jew, It's Jesus

ONE DAY A CHILD by the name of Joshua bar Joseph was born in Bethlehem, a small village just south of Jerusalem. The boy was the firstborn of the family so he was circumcised on the eighth day after his birth, as the Law of Moses required. Another requirement of the law for the firstborn was that the parents were to make an atoning sacrifice, since everything that is firstborn belongs to God. Being such a poor family, the exchange this boy's parents made was that of two doves. In his hometown of Nazareth, Joshua grew up in a typical Jewish environment. He was enrolled in school along with the other Jewish boys. He was instructed by rabbis in the synagogue and the textbook they used was what is today the Old Testament. Upon completion of their schooling, most of the students could recite long portions of the texts in the Pentateuch, Psalms and Prophets by heart.

Joshua was such a good student that one day, when he had joined his parents on a visit to Jerusalem during Passover, he stayed behind and discussed Scriptures about the Law of Moses with the teachers of the law in the temple. He was only twelve years old.

Joshua grew up in a time when Rome was expanding. Nazareth was a small, insignificant place, but ten km to the north was the big city of Zipporah, the residential city of Galilee and Peree. That city was bustling and teeming with life, and Joshua most likely visited it often with his parents.

**Jesus the Jew**
*Joshua bar Joseph*, or in English *Joshua son of Joseph*, is Greek for "Jesus." Jesus was a Jew. He grew up as a Jew and shared in his people's customs, rituals and spiritual inheritance. Nowhere in the New Testament is there the slightest mention of Jesus giving up his Jewish identity. He was born as a Jew, lived as a Jew and was buried as a Jew. John writes that *"he came to His own,"* that is the Jews (John 1:11). He came, Paul writes, born under the Law of Moses. *"But when the fullness of the time had come, God sent forth His Son, born of a woman, born under the law"* (Gal. 4:4).

Jesus personally confirms this for his disciples when he declares: *"Do not think that I came to destroy the Law or the Prophets; I have not come to destroy but to fulfill"* (Matt. 5:17). He came to fulfill, meaning that Jesus did not break a single one of the 613 commands in the Law of Moses. That leads us to the conclusion that if anyone has ever been a Jew, then it was Jesus. In him the law and teaching of Moses were personified and fulfilled.

**The most important commandment**
*"A new commandment I give to you,"* he said to his disciples, *"that you love one another"* (John 13:34). Some people make the mistake of using this command as a way of elevating Jesus above the Law of Moses or separating him from it. That is completely wrong. When Jesus hears the question about the most important commandment, he answers in the same way all Jews always have. He quotes the most central text in the whole Bible, the *"shema,"* which is the Jewish state-

ment of faith. No Bible passage has been read more often than this one, since it is quoted morning and night in the synagogue, as well as on many other occasions:

> *Hear, O Israel: The LORD our God, the LORD is one! You shall love the LORD your God with all your heart, with all your soul, and with all your strength. And these words which I command you today shall be in your heart. You shall teach them diligently to your children, and shall talk of them when you sit in your house, when you walk by the way, when you lie down, and when you rise up. You shall bind them as a sign on your hand, and they shall be as frontlets between your eyes. You shall write them on the doorposts of your house and on your gates.* Deuteronomy 6:4–9

When Jesus quotes the *"shema"* in Mark 12:29–31, he identifies himself literally with Judaism and with the Law of Moses.

### "You shall not shave around the sides of your head"

What did Jesus look like? No one knows for sure, but we can be fairly certain that none of the many paintings that hang in our churches and homes even come close. He had brown eyes, and if you have been in Israel you have surely noticed that the Hasidic* orthodox Jews do not cut their hair at the temples, but that it hangs in long, curled sideburns down the sides of the Jew's face. But did Jesus have these sideburns? Maybe. According to the Hasidic tradition, different passages of the Old Testament about not shaving or cutting at the side of the head are interpreted to mean that the hair at the temples should be allowed to grow long.

> *You shall not shave around the sides of your head, nor shall you disfigure the edges of your beard.* Leviticus 19:27

### "You are to make tassels on the corners of your garments"

One day when Jesus was surrounded by a bustling crowd, a woman

## PART II — THE PEOPLE, THE LAND, THE CITY AND THE TASK

in desperate need of relief from her physical suffering pushed her way forward toward the man she had heard so much about. *"And suddenly, a woman who had a flow of blood for twelve years came from behind and touched the hem of His garment"* (Matt. 9:20). It says that the woman was healed when she touched the hem of Jesus' garment. But what was on the hem of Jesus' garment?

> *Again the LORD spoke to Moses, saying, "Speak to the children of Israel: Tell them to make tassels on the corners of their garments throughout their generations, and to put a blue thread in the tassels of the corners. And you shall have the tassel, that you may look upon it and remember all the commandments of the LORD and do them, and that you may not follow the harlotry to which your own heart and your own eyes are inclined, and that you may remember and do all My commandments, and be holy for your God. I am the LORD your God, who brought you out of the land of Egypt, to be your God: I am the LORD your God."* Numbers 15:37–41

Since the time of Moses, Jews have used a special prayer shawl called a tallit. The prayer shawl was in general use at the time of Jesus and was worn outside the outer clothing. The corner tassels that the woman touched were on this shawl. The tassels' appearance has a symbolic meaning. They consist of eight threads that are woven into five knots. In Hebrew the corner tassels are called "tzitzit." The letters in "tzitzit" have a value of six hundred in Hebrew. If we add eight for the eight threads and five for the five knots we get the number 613, which is also the number of commands in the Pentateuch.

There is a message in this story. The woman touched the corner tassels of Jesus' garment. What did the corner tassels symbolize? They symbolized Judaism, the Old Testament and the teaching of Moses. When the woman touched Jesus, she was touching Jesus the Jew.

## "Bind them as a sign on your hand"

*You shall bind them as a sign on your hand, and they shall be as frontlets between your eyes. You shall write them on the doorposts of your house and on your gates.* Deuteronomy 6:8–9

In order to obey the command of having a symbol on the hand and forehead as a reminder of God's law, leather straps with boxes were attached to the forehead and upper arm. The boxes were made of ox skin and contained texts from the Pentateuch (see Ex. 13:1–10, Deut. 6:4–9 and 11:13–21).

These phylacteries were called *"tefillin"* and wrapped seven times around the left underarm. Left-handed men tie it on the right arm since, according to tradition, it should be wrapped on *"the weak hand"* (compare Ex. 13:16). They are tied only on weekdays since the Sabbath in itself is a sign (see Ex. 31:17). The use of tefillin first begins when a boy turns thirteen and one day. In the New Testament, phylacteries are only mentioned once. Jesus did not have anything against tefillin, and probably used them himself since he did fulfill the law. But he was against those who puffed themselves up by making exclusive phylacteries (see Matt. 23:5).

## "The burial cloth was folded up by itself"

When Jesus was buried it was a typical Jewish burial. When John and Peter, after the resurrection, came to the opening of the tomb and looked in, they noticed that the burial cloth was not lying among the linen, but folded up by itself. *"... and the handkerchief that had been around His head, not lying with the linen cloths, but folded together in a place by itself"* (John 20:7). I have wondered about a few things concerning this Bible verse. First, why was it written that it was lying folded? Second, why did Jesus take time to fold the burial cloth at the resurrection? Why even mention a burial cloth in this context? But the cloth that is written about in the gospel of John was something far more than a normal burial cloth. It was a tallit, a prayer shawl. It had symbolic meaning and symbolized the law. When a Jew is buried, he is buried with his tallit. It is folded according to tradition and placed over the dead man's face, which according to my learned Jewish friend Shraga means that you die as a free man under the Law of Moses. Of course Jesus would never, not even in the event of his resurrection, make light of this symbolism. I don't know if it was Jesus or the angels who folded the prayer shawl, but I do know that Jesus was buried as a Jew, as "a free man under the Law of Moses."

Jesus was a Jew. He grew up among his people, the Jews, he dressed as a Jew, and he probably had long curly sideburns hanging from his temples. When he prayed he put on a prayer shawl, touching the corner tassels and lifting his arm, on which the phylacteries, the tefillin, were wrapped. On his forehead was fastened a small box in which parts of Moses' teaching were written.

"Obey the teachers of the law and do everything they tell you," he taught his disciples. *"But do not live the way they live, for they do not practice what they preach"* (see Matt. 23:1-3). Jesus never broke the law, but he did teach against hypocrisy and against any interpretation of the Law of Moses that twisted the Law into becoming a burden for the people while giving advantages to the religious elite.

Jesus loved his Jewish people. A few days before his death, as he was sitting on the Mount of Olives, he wept with love for his people. He looked prophetically into the future and saw the suffering "his own" would have to go through. But he also gave a sharp warning to all other nations. "Whatever you did for one of the least of these brothers of mine, you did to me." That is to say that whatever we do to the Jews, we are also doing to Jesus. He is of the tribe of Judah, so the Jewish people will always be his brothers (see Matt. 25).

## The first generation of Christians

The first generation of Christians was made up of Jews, and they saw themselves as a part of Israel, living a life loyal to their Jewish heritage. Peter reacted aggressively when he saw unclean animals coming down from heaven in a vision and heard God's voice speak to him and say "Kill and eat." His reply was, *"Not so, Lord! I have never eaten anything common or unclean"* (Acts 10:14). Why did Peter react so strongly? Because the teachings he had heard from Jesus were always consistent with the Law.

It took visions and visits from angels in order to change his opinion, and it was against his will that Peter agreed to visit Cornelius the Gentile's house. Going in under the roof of a Gentile meant ritual uncleanliness to Peter. When the Holy Spirit fell upon Cornelius the Gentile and his entire Gentile family, Peter was probably just as surprised as they were (see Acts 10).

In Jerusalem the church leadership reacted severely. "What have you done, Peter?" the church leaders asked. "You don't mean that you preached the gospel of Christ to the Gentiles?" Peter was questioned intensely (see Acts 11:1–18). Apparently the disciples had not understood that the gospel would be preached to all nations. "But," someone might say, "Jesus does say 'to all nations.'" Yes, but only on a few occasions and even then in the Jewish context. It may have been so that it wasn't until the Holy Spirit fell on Pentecost that Jesus' disciples began to understand the extent and greatness of Jesus' commission to them (see John 16:12–13).

Would the Gentiles be forced to become Jews in order to become Christians? This question, addressed at a major church meeting in Jerusalem in the year 49, is irrelevant today but still worth taking a look at. The question did not have to do with whether Jews who had come to faith in Jesus could still live as Jews and follow the Law of Moses. That was considered obvious. Instead, the question had to do with whether Gentiles who had been saved should also submit to the Law of Moses. Does a Gentile who comes to faith in Jesus also have to convert and become a Jew in order to be saved? What were the regulations for a Gentile who had come to faith in Jesus to even be allowed to become a part of the church? Could you get "saved" without being a part of God's own people, the Jews? And could you be a part of Jesus' church without placing yourself under the Law of Moses?

The very core of the leaders of the Christian movement had gathered in Jerusalem. Some claimed that no one could be welcomed into Jesus' church if they had not also converted to Judaism; meaning getting circumcised, changing their eating habits and submitting to all of the commands in Moses' teaching.

This issue was enormous and it ended up causing division in the churches. On the one hand it was obvious to the Jews that Gentiles couldn't become "Christians." Throughout the entire Old Testament God had commanded that the Jews were forbidden from getting mixed up with and associating with other peoples. That is why it was so imperative that Jesus, who was God come in the flesh, should not deviate from Moses' teachings. But on the other hand, the Holy Spirit was falling upon the Gentiles when they came to faith, with the same power and manifestations as when the Holy Spirit was falling upon the Jews.

When we read today about how a decision was reached, it is hard for us to understand how monumental that decision was, since the members of the Jewish church really were Jews. They loved and followed the Jew Jesus, who was the Jews' God come in the flesh. I must say that I admire the leaders in Jerusalem who were bold enough to make the decision they made.

After lengthy discussions the apostles and the elders, in consultation with the Holy Spirit, decided that the Gentiles who were saved did not have to become "Jews" in order to become Christians. But in order to live at peace with the churches, a compromise was reached. The Gentile Christians would not:
- Eat meat that was unclean through idol worship
- Commit adultery
- Eat meat from suffocated animals
- Eat food with blood in it

## A ten-thousand-member Jewish church, affirmed by Paul
When Paul visited Jerusalem for the last time in 58 A.D., he came to a large church with tens of thousands of members. He came to the

original church, the mother of churches, and everyone was a Jew and held firmly to the Law of Moses.

> "On the following day Paul went in with us to James, and all the elders were present. When he had greeted them, he told in detail those things which God had done among the Gentiles through his ministry. And when they heard it, they glorified the Lord. And they said to him, " You see, brother, how many myriads of Jews there are who have believed, and they are all zealous for the law; but they have been informed about you that you teach all the Jews who are among the Gentiles to forsake Moses, saying that they ought not to circumcise their children nor to walk according to the customs. What then? The assembly must certainly meet, for they will hear that you have come. Therefore do what we tell you: We have four men who have taken a vow. Take them and be purified with them, and pay their expenses so that they may shave their heads, and that all may know that those things of which they were informed concerning you are nothing, but that you yourself also walk orderly and keep the law." Acts 21:18–24

We can see here that despite the church meeting that had taken place ten years previously, the Christian Jews in Jerusalem had a very hard time accepting that Gentiles could become Christians. But we should notice even more carefully the reaction of Paul, who—without objecting—entered into the strictest possible observance of the Torah in order to truly show that he identified himself with the Law of Moses and with the Jews.

The strange thing about the development of church history is that the original problem was whether the Gentiles could even be accepted in Christ. However, only 300 years later, this same issue was approached from the opposite angle: Jews were not allowed into the Christian church and Jewish Christians were made to reject the Law of Moses.

One thing that might explain this abrupt turnaround is that

Christianity's Jewish roots were replaced with a culture of idol worship at the end of the 200s. During the latter phase of early church history, many things were introduced that were completely foreign to the Christians of the first generation. Maybe that was why they wanted to do away with any Jewish identity: so that the Christian faith could be infiltrated by the evils of the religions of the Gentiles. A Jewish Christian would never have gone along with introducing the Mary cult into their faith, appointing the papacy, practicing celibacy, teaching transubstantiation, etc. Such a seduction of the church would not have even been tolerated if the church had maintained its Jewish roots. That day in 325 when the church decided to "separate from the detestable company of the Jews" is the day the church destroyed itself.

**Together with the Jews in the eternity of eternities**

> *Then one of the seven angels who had the seven bowls filled with the seven last plagues came to me and talked with me, saying, "Come, I will show you the bride, the Lamb's wife." And he carried me away in the Spirit to a great and high mountain, and showed me the great city, the holy Jerusalem, descending out of heaven from God, having the glory of God. Her light was like a most precious stone, like a jasper stone, clear as crystal. Also she had a great and high wall with twelve gates, and twelve angels at the gates, and names written on them, which are the names of the twelve tribes of the children of Israel: three gates on the east, three gates on the north, three gates on the south, and three gates on the west. Now the wall of the city had twelve foundations, and on them were the names of the twelve apostles of the Lamb.* Revelation 21:9–14

As we can read and understand, the Jew is absolutely central in the New Testament and in the eschatological final phase of time. The Jew Jesus will reveal himself and come back to his people the Jews. The Jewish Jerusalem will be the center for these events. And God's eternal temple will always remind us that the Jewish people are the chosen ones, since the names of the twelve tribes of Israel will be engraved on the gates of the temple, and the names of the Jewish apostles are written on the city's foundation stones. If you are planning to spend eternity in the kingdom of God it would be wise to consider these truths, since it would be a terrible "fate" to be reminded of how wrong you were for an eternity of eternities. ✡

## Israel, The Land Of Promise

THE FIRST TIME I arrived in Israel, it was as the leader of a Christian pilgrim group from Sweden. I was amazed to discover that what I considered to be Israel was no longer called Israel but the West Bank. Half of Jerusalem, all of Bethlehem, Bethany, Shechem, Jericho and Hebron—the heart of the land that God promised Abraham and the core of the kingdom that David built—were and are today the West Bank. The places where Jesus ministered and what all Christians associate with the land of Canaan, the promised land or the land of Jesus, are today under Palestinian rule. According to the United Nations, Israel has illegally occupied the West Bank since the war of 1967. But if we had called the West Bank by its historical name, Judea and Samaria, then the word "occupation" would have taken on a completely different meaning since most of us admit that Judea is, historically, the land of the Jews. The truth is that it is not the Jews who have occupied West Bank; it is Islam that has occupied Judea.

# PART II — THE PEOPLE, THE LAND, THE CITY AND THE TASK

For believers—whether Jewish or Christian—it is hard to deny the connection between the Jews and the land of Israel. Throughout the entire Bible the promises from God to the Jewish people about the land of Israel are repeated over and over again. Jesus foretold the destruction of Jerusalem (see Luke 21:20–24), but he also foretold the Jewish people's return to Israel and Jerusalem. In John's Revelation, the book that concludes the New Testament and is a portrayal of the end times, the Jewish people, the land of Israel and the city of Jerusalem are one single and obvious entity.

## The eternal promises about the land

*Abram passed through the land to the place of Shechem, as far as the terebinth tree of Moreh. And the Canaanites were then in the land. Then the LORD appeared to Abram and said, "To your descendants I will give this land." And there he built an altar to the LORD, who had appeared to him.* Genesis 12:6–7

The first time Abraham enters the land of Canaan, he receives a fantastic promise from God. This land would be given to Abraham's descendants, the Jewish people. Several years later, after the journey to Egypt, Abraham meets with God again. On one of the mountaintops surrounding Jerusalem, God renews his promises about the land. It is morning and the sun has just risen. The fog has dissipated and God speaks to Abraham and asks him to take a look around. Abraham looks to the north and glimpses Mt. Hermon's snow-capped peaks on the horizon. He sees Carmel to the northwest, the Mediterranean Sea to the far west, the river Jordan, Jericho, the land east of Jordan, and the dry deserts of Judea to the south.

"All of this land that you see now," God whispers to Abraham, "I give to you and to your descendants."

Abraham is amazed at the thought. It is a great land, a rich country that has everything anyone could ask for.

"And," God whispers, "it's yours forever!"

"Forever," Abraham thinks. "That must mean that my descendants will live here forever."

Abraham then moves throughout the land, building altars, calling on the name of the Lord, and then when he arrives at Hebron, he settles.

*"All the land which you see I give to you and your descendants forever ... Arise, walk in the land through its length and its width, for I give it to you." Then Abram moved his tent, and went and dwelt by the terebinth trees of Mamre, which are in Hebron, and built an altar there to the LORD.* Genesis 13:15, 17–18

## The borders of the land

*On the same day the LORD made a covenant with Abram, saying: "To your descendants I have given this land, from the river of Egypt to the great river, the River Euphrates—the Kenites, the Kenezzites, the Kadmonites, the Hittites, the Perizzites, the Rephaim, the Amorites, the Canaanites, the Girgashites, and the Jebusites."* Genesis 15:18–21

So where should the borders of Israel be? In verse 6, which precedes the quote above, it says: *"Abram believed the Lord, and He accounted it to him for righteousness."* Faith is one of the central themes of the Bible. The great thing about Abraham, which distinguished him from many of the other people of his day, was that he really did believe. He experienced God's being, he dreamed, and the images that God gave him became living visions. He was able to imagine how the whole land he had seen one morning would one day belong to his descendants. But God was more precise and he also told Abraham which geographic borders the land would have. The borders above have been the object of much discussion, since there are many ways to interpret the border to the great river Euphrates. If it meant the distant portion of the Euphrates, then the eastern border of Israel would stretch to Kuwait, include Lebanon, Syria, all of Jordan and the Sinai desert, all the way down to the Nile. However, the borders can also be interpreted to mean land that is a bit smaller. It was as if God was saying: "Your faith will set the border. The size of the land can end at any part of the Euphrates; it's up to your faith."

## The promise of the land: something God will never forget

> *"Remember Abraham, Isaac, and Israel, Your servants, to whom You swore by Your own self, and said to them, 'I will multiply your descendants as the stars of heaven; and all this land that I have spoken of I give to your descendants, and they shall inherit it forever.'" So the LORD relented from the harm which He said He would do to His people.* Exodus 32:13–14

The covenant that God entered into with Abraham was also very powerful. When the entire Jewish nation returned from slavery in Egypt 600 years later, it was because of the covenant. When they rebelled against both God and Moses despite what God had done, it was this covenant with Abraham that Moses called upon to prevent God's wrath to destroy the people.

> *He remembers His covenant forever, the word which He commanded, for a thousand generations, the covenant which He made with Abraham, and His oath to Isaac, and confirmed it to Jacob for a statute, to Israel as an everlasting covenant, saying, "To you I will give the land of Canaan as the allotment of your inheritance," when they were few in number, indeed very few, and strangers in it. When they went from one nation to another, from one kingdom to another people …* Psalm 105:8–13

Today, it is incredibly important to be aware of these Bible verses (and many others), and to emphasize them in the debate that is raging about Israel's right to exist as a country and which geographic borders are correct. It is also extremely important to point out these Biblical statements to other Christians, since there are many who have no relevant Biblical teaching on this matter. Think about it! Christianity lays claim to all of the Old Testament promises relating to salvation and the forgiveness of sins. And if God himself expressly says that these promises are eternal, then how can a church or a Christian claim anything other than that God's eternal promises to Israel must also be true? Meaning that the area of land that is today Jordan, Lebanon, the West Bank and parts of Syria are Israel and belong to the Jewish people?

**The Jews have the historical, theological and legal right to the land and to the city**
There is no other country in the world where the association between the people and the land is as strong as it is for Israel. It is not because of the Jews that there hasn't been a Jewish state for 2,000 years; it is because the occupying power there has been too powerful. The Jews have been forbidden to live in Israel from the year 135. They came in illegally anyway, and rich Jews bought themselves in. During these past 2,000 years, the small Jewish groups in the land have been subject to continual pogroms, and yet they refused to surrender and leave. Even though most of them have lived outside of their land for 2,000 years, the Jews have refused to give up the dream of one day returning and restoring the kingdom of David.

What is strange is that even though the Jewish people have been forced from their land twice, there is hardly another people in history more associated with their land than what the Jews are. It is the same with Jerusalem. There are many who make a claim on Jerusalem, but the truth is that Jerusalem has never been any other people's capital city than the Jews. So the first conclusion is that the Jewish people have a historical right to the land and the city.

The second conclusion is that the Jewish people have a theological right to the land. This view is a part of the whole point of this book: there has never been a people more theologically associated with a place than the Jews are with Israel. Even the Jews' most adamant opponents know this. That is why Islam is doing everything it can to remove every trace of the Jewish temple from the Temple Mount.

There is another relevant connection that can be made, and that is the legal one. What is interesting in this context is that the most controversial places in this conflict—Jerusalem, Hebron, and Shechem—were actually already bought by a Jew for Jews, with contracts of purchase that can be found in the Bible. Abraham bought Hebron from the Hittite Ephron:

*So the field of Ephron which was in Machpelah which was before Mamre, the field and the cave which was in it, and all the trees that were in the field, which were within all the surrounding borders, were deeded to Abraham.* Genesis 23:17

Jacob bought Shechem, modern-day Nablus, from Hamor's sons:

*Then Jacob came safely to the city of Shechem, which is in the land of Canaan, when he came from Padan Aram; and he pitched his tent before the city. And he bought the parcel of land, where he had pitched his tent, from the children of Hamor, Shechem's father, for one hundred pieces of money. Then he erected an altar there and called it El Elohe Israel."* Genesis 33:18–20

David bought the temple site, the heart of Jerusalem, from the Jebusite Araunah:

*So the LORD sent a plague upon Israel from the morning till the appointed time. From Dan to Beersheba seventy thousand men of the people died. And when the angel stretched out His hand over Jerusalem to destroy it, the LORD relented from the destruction, and said to the angel who was destroying the people, "It is enough; now restrain your hand." And the angel of the LORD was by the threshing floor of Araunah the Jebusite. Then*

*David spoke to the LORD when he saw the angel who was striking the people, and said, "Surely I have sinned, and I have done wickedly; but these sheep, what have they done? Let Your hand, I pray, be against me and against my father's house." And Gad came that day to David and said to him, "Go up, erect an altar to the LORD on the threshing floor of Araunah the Jebusite." So David, according to the word of Gad, went up as the LORD commanded. Now Araunah looked, and saw the king and his servants coming toward him. So Araunah went out and bowed before the king with his face to the ground. Then Araunah said, " Why has my lord the king come to his servant?" And David said, "To buy the threshing floor from you, to build an altar to the LORD, that the plague may be withdrawn from the people." Now Araunah said to David, "Let my lord the king take and offer up whatever seems good to him. Look, here are oxen for burnt sacrifice, and threshing implements and the yokes of the oxen for wood. All these, O king, Araunah has given to the king." And Araunah said to the king, "May the LORD your God accept you." Then the king said to Araunah, "No, but I will surely buy it from you for a price; nor will I offer burnt offerings to the LORD my God with that which costs me nothing." So David bought the threshing floor and the oxen for fifty shekels of silver. And David built there an altar to the LORD, and offered burnt offerings and peace offerings. So the LORD heeded the prayers for the land, and the plague was withdrawn from Israel.* 2 Samuel 24:15–25

In conclusion, we can establish that the Bible verifies that the Jewish people's forefathers—Abraham 3,800 years ago, Jacob 100 years later and David about 900 B.C.—bought the central places in Israel where the conflict is the most intense today. What may surprise many is that there is a legal connection, a written contract, between the Jews and the land of Israel. It's all in the Bible.

But all of these places—where the eternal promises about the land were made, where borders were promised, where financial contracts verified ownership, and where all of the Biblical figures from Abraham to Jesus walked and recognized Israel as the land of the Jews—all of these are today the West Bank. There are no synagogues or churches here. There is no religious freedom here. In Jericho, Bethany, Shechem, Bethel, Bethlehem and even in eastern Jerusalem, you cannot openly talk about Jesus. Here Islam reigns in its strictest form. Those who have converted to Christianity do so at a risk to their lives. The Israel that many Westerners romantically dream of is today the land of the Islamic priests, the mullahs. They have declared war (intifada) against Christianity and the Jews. They have built their own temple on Mt. Moriah, the place where Abraham was going to sacrifice Isaac, the threshing floor David purchased, and where Solomon built the first temple. This is also where Jesus taught the people. And yet Jews aren't even allowed to set foot here! The event that triggered the intifada in 2001 was when Israel's prime minister Ariel Sharon visited this place.

In the debate that is going on in the media today, Israel is accused of occupying the West Bank. But that is an accusation with no historical basis. It isn't the Jews who have occupied Judea and Samaria; it is Islam that has occupied the promised land. ✡

# 8

## The People, The Land, The City, And The Task

**WHY DOESN'T ANYONE** fight over the southern province of Sweden, for example? At one time they actually did! In the 1600s the countries located around the Baltic Sea battled regularly for political power over the harbors connecting the sea to the land. From these ports, boats could move up the rivers and into the countries where they could trade and do business.

When the Swedish army, a long way from home, secured its territory in what is today northern Poland, the Danish king declared war against Sweden, attacking a defenseless nation. The Swedish king, Carl Gustav the 10th, decided to take a big risk at that point. In the middle of the night on January 30, 1658, he gave marching orders. He had to take a shortcut. With his entire army he crossed over the frozen Baltic Sea on the creaking ice. A week later he took control of Copenhagen in Denmark with the entire Swedish army.

## PART II — THE PEOPLE, THE LAND, THE CITY AND THE TASK

The Danes were forced into checkmate. If it hadn't been for the threats of Holland and England to attack Sweden if they conquered Denmark, then all of Denmark might have been Swedish today! Instead, the Danes were forced to purchase peace with the Swedes, and the price was the land of southern Sweden.

A resistance movement called the snapphanes was formed in what is now southern Sweden, but after a few decades of guerrilla warfare the snapphanes were defeated and fairly soon the part of Sweden that was under Danish rule up until 1658 was absorbed by Sweden, a superpower of that time.

In one of the boldest moves in European war history, the Swedish king bet everything on a single card. The thickness of the ice across the sound on that unusually cold winter changed the Scandinavian map forever. However, even though that was a mere 350 years ago, there is not a single Swede who is fighting to get southern Sweden united with Denmark again. A similar scenario can be found in many places in the world. They all follow the same pattern: a guerrilla movement rises up and fights for a few decades, but if the political power of the conqueror is strong and stable, the population will, within a century, be absorbed into the "new" nation.

### There's always an exception to the rule

But there is one exception. The Jews have never been absorbed by anyone anywhere, and the land of Israel has never been the land of another people. Even though the Jews have been away from their land for 2,000 years, no other people group has declared a national state there! Jerusalem, with its strategic location on the plot of land between three continents, has never been the capital city of another people. In other parts of the world the political maps are being redrawn and people groups are being absorbed and assimilated. Everything seems to be in a state of change. Everything except Israel.

On two occasions the entire people have been deported or driven away from the land. The first instance was during the time of the Babylonian superpower in the 500s B.C. Even though a small group of Jews had begun to return to Israel after seventy years in exile, the real re-immigration didn't get underway until a few decades later. But even though the Jews were basically absent from the land for close to 100 years, there was no other people group who claimed the land, much less claimed the city of Jerusalem, a city that lay in ruins when Nehemiah returned in 445 B.C. to seriously deal with the rebuilding of Jerusalem.

The second occasion was in 135 A.D., when Rome turned back a widespread revolt against the occupying superpower. All of Jerusalem was torn down and a new city, Aelia Capitolina, replaced the old one. It was forbidden for any Jews to be found in the land, putting into effect an excommunication that would last nearly 2,000 years. But throughout all of these years, there was no other group that took over the land, even though there were plenty of Bedouin tribes (nomadic people who moved from place to place).

None of the people or armies who fought over Jerusalem during the Crusades made it their capital city either. So why didn't anyone ever annex and incorporate the land that everyone thinks is so valuable today? It's because when the Jews aren't in the land, Israel withers. Jerusalem's beauty wastes away and the land is transformed into a desert. Mark Twain wrote the following when he visited the land in 1867: "The promised land has lost all its glory." And that is true. After the Jews were forced to leave the land in the year 135, all of the vegetation began to wither. The land dried up, and after a few centuries no one could live there anymore. So when the first Russian Zionists began to return to Israel at the end of the 1800s, what they came to was a desert and a wilderness. But through diligent work and with godly intuition they dug forth the ancient wells, and the wilderness was transformed into fertile fields and the desert began to bloom.

"But," someone may ask, "what about the Palestinians? Haven't they been there the whole time?" No, the Palestinians came when the Jews did. When the Jews returned to Israel, it meant an increase in the welfare of the land. As the Zionists cultivated the land, new societies with functional health care were established, something the

Bedouin tribes were in great need of. At the same time, the Jews needed more laborers. The truth is that it was the Zionists who recolonized Israel at the end of the 1800s. Paradoxically, the Jews needed the Arab workforce and the Arabs needed the Jews' welfare. Today Israel is a veritable cornucopia. The land that was a desert only 150 years ago now boasts six million people. How is this possible? The answer is that the land and the people belong together. The land was created for the people and the people for the land. When they are together they both flourish.

**One people, created for one land**
To understand the connection between the land and the people we have to return to Moses and his final words to the people before the Lord took him home. After forty years in the desert, Israel was now finally at the edge of their new land. In his final speech to them, Moses summarizes the teaching he has personally received from God. He imprints the commands on their minds and reminds them of the miracles the Lord has performed during their wanderings in the desert. In his speech, which basically makes up the entire book of Deuteronomy, there is also a description of the benefits of hearing the voice of the Lord and obeying it, as well as the consequences if the people do not obey and do not walk in the covenant that they willingly and collectively entered into with God.

> *If you diligently obey the voice of the LORD your God, to observe carefully all His commandments which I command you today, that the LORD your God will set you high above all nations of the earth. And all these blessings shall come upon you and overtake you, because you obey the voice of the LORD your God: Blessed shall you be in the city, and blessed shall you be in the country. Blessed shall be the fruit of your body, the produce of your ground and the increase of your herds, the increase of your cattle and the offspring of your flocks. Blessed shall be your basket and your kneading bowl. Blessed shall you be when you*

*come in, and blessed shall you be when you go out. The LORD will cause your enemies who rise against you to be defeated before your face; they shall come out against you one way and flee before you seven ways. The LORD will command the blessing on you in your storehouses and in all to which you set your hand, and He will bless you in the land which the LORD your God is giving you. The LORD will establish you as a holy people to Himself, just as He has sworn to you, if you keep the commandments of the LORD your God and walk in His ways. Then all peoples of the earth shall see that you are called by the name of the LORD, and they shall be afraid of you. And the LORD will grant you plenty of goods, in the fruit of your body, in the increase of your livestock, and in the produce of your ground, in the land of which the LORD swore to your fathers to give you. The LORD will open to you His good treasure, the heavens, to give the rain to your land in its season, and to bless all the work of your hand. You shall lend to many nations, but you shall not borrow. And the LORD will make you the head and not the tail; you shall be above only, and not be beneath, if you heed the commandments of the LORD your God, which I command you today, and are careful to observe them. So you shall not turn aside from any of the words which I command you this day, to the right or the left, to go after other gods to serve them.* Deuteronomy 28:1–14

These first fourteen verses of Deuteronomy 28 are fantastic. The Jewish people would have total success in the land that the Lord gave to them. They would be blessed in everything, everywhere. Whatever they did would prosper and they would live in an abundance of everything good. They would never have to borrow and no enemy would have a shadow of a chance against them. There is even the promise of a perfect climate—the heavens would provide rain at the right time. However, there were two conditions. Success was promised if the Jewish people obeyed the Lord in everything.

## PART II — THE PEOPLE, THE LAND, THE CITY AND THE TASK

**When the people are in the Diaspora, the land becomes a desert**
But if they did not obey, a curse would come over the Jewish people and over the land. Fourteen verses that promised total prosperity are followed by fifty-four verses that accurately describe what would happen—and what then really did happen—if the Jewish people turned their backs on the Lord their God. This is a dire passage, and later on we will touch on some of the statements that are made.

But what does the curse have to do with the land? Quite a lot, since the land and the people are one! When the people are in the land, both the people and the land flourish, and when the people are driven from the land—because they haven't obeyed the Lord—then both wither.

> *The coming generation of your children who rise up after you, and the foreigner who comes from a far land, would say, when they see the plagues of that land and the sicknesses which the LORD has laid on it: The whole land is brimstone, salt, and burning; it is not sown, nor does it bear, nor does any grass grow there, like the overthrow of Sodom and Gomorrah, Admah, and Zeboiim, which the LORD overthrew in His anger and His wrath. All nations would say, ' Why has the LORD done so to this land? What does the heat of this great anger mean?' Then people would say: 'Because they have forsaken the covenant of the LORD God of their fathers, which He made with them when He brought them out of the land of Egypt."* Deuteronomy 29:22–25

There is a pattern that follows the entire history of the Jewish people. When the Jews serve the Lord their God and obey the covenant, they also release the promised blessing, all according to the covenant they have entered into with God.

But when the people, for different reasons, turn away from God, curses are released instead, and the people are then driven from the land. When the people are not in the land, the curse goes into effect, all according to the last part of Deuteronomy 28. In the Diaspora the people have no peace, no place to rest their feet, and they are forced to continually break camp and move on to new places. Everywhere they are misunderstood, blamed and ridiculed. They are forced to move from country to country. In the beginning of the 1900s the Jews had spread all across the world. There was nowhere left on earth to escape to.

> *You shall be plucked from off the land which you go to possess. Then the LORD will scatter you among all peoples, from one end of the earth to the other, and there you shall serve other gods, which neither you nor your fathers have known—wood and stone. And among those nations you shall find no rest, nor shall the sole of your foot have a resting place; but there the LORD will give you a trembling heart, failing eyes, and anguish of soul. Your life shall hang in doubt before you; you shall fear day and night, and have no assurance of life. In the morning you shall say, 'Oh, that it were evening!' And at evening you shall say, 'Oh, that it were morning!' because of the fear which terrifies your heart, and because of the sight which your eyes see.*
> Deuteronomy 28:63b–67

## The covenant is eternal and restoration is always near

> *When all these things come upon you, the blessing and the curse which I have set before you, and you call them to mind among all the nations where the LORD your God drives you, and you return to the LORD your God and obey His voice, according to all that I command you today, you and your children, with all your heart and with all your soul, that the LORD your God will bring you back from captivity, and have compassion on you, and gather you again from all the nations where the LORD your God has scattered you. If any of you are driven out to the farthest parts under heaven, from there the LORD your God will gather you, and from there He will bring you. Then the LORD your God*

> *will bring you to the land which your fathers possessed, and you shall possess it. He will prosper you and multiply you more than your fathers. The LORD your God will make you abound in all the work of your hand, in the fruit of your body, in the increase of your livestock, and in the produce of your land for good. For the LORD will again rejoice over you for good as He rejoiced over your fathers.* Deuteronomy 30:1–5,9

According to the Bible, the Jews as a people and the geographical land of Israel have a unique relationship with God. For those on the outside—Christians, atheists, Muslims—this relationship and the covenant fellowship will always evoke admiration. The land has a life of its own; it becomes fertile when the people return, and it changes from desert to lush soil that is flowing with milk and honey.

What many have forgotten throughout history is that despite the tough times that the Jews have gone through, they are still the Lord's precious possession. With an eternal love and deep passion, God loves the people and the land. Even if they are driven to the ends of the earth, he will still gather them to Israel and bless them with all of his abundance when they return to live in the covenant.

No people and no church can ever take Israel's place in God's heart. No one can replace their right to or belonging to the land. As long as the sun is appointed to shine, the Jewish people will be the Lord's chosen.

> *The LORD has appeared of old to me, saying: " Yes, I have loved you with an everlasting love; therefore with lovingkindness I have drawn you" ... Thus says the LORD, who gives the sun for a light by day, the ordinances of the moon and the stars for a light by night, who disturbs the sea, and its waves roar (the LORD of hosts is His name): "If those ordinances depart from before Me, says the LORD, then the seed of Israel shall also cease from being a nation before Me forever."* Jeremiah 31:3, 35–36

## The task is a part of the people and of the land

We started the chapter by discussing Denmark and the lands of southern Sweden. We saw how the Danish population, after Denmark's surrender, gave up and then assimilated into Sweden after about a century. But the history of Israel and of the Jews looks different. What is it that makes Israel, Jerusalem and the Jewish people different from all other people, cities and lands? What is it that will always make the Jewish people, the land and the city different?

That question has a theological answer. In the covenant that God and Abraham made with one another, there was a plan of salvation for the entire world. In accordance with the Old Testament, the salvation of the world will come from the Jews the day that the Messiah comes and restores his kingdom of peace.

Their task was to birth the Messiah. The people that God chose would be a holy people, a people of priests, a people who were set apart for a fantastic task. That place was Israel, a land that flowed with milk and honey and that gave rain at the right time. Here the living God would one day become a man and walk among us all, and then in the city of Jerusalem freely give his life for all of mankind, as a perfect sacrifice. When Abraham traveled with his only son Isaac to Jerusalem and Mt. Moriah to sacrifice him in faithfulness to God, it was a test that would be a shadow of the covenant, when God the Father himself would one day sacrifice his son in the same place that Abraham raised his knife to offer up his son Isaac as a blood sacrifice. So there was—beyond political motives—a spiritual explanation for why the rulers of ancient times fought over Israel, why Pharaoh sought a way to eradicate the Jews, why the wandering in the wilderness took forty years, and why Israel has been occupied time and time again. There is a spiritual perspective to the conflict that is the result of God having chosen a people, a land and a city where he would come down to us as a man and freely give his life in exchange for us all.

"But," someone may ask, "all of this has already happened. Why is there still fighting over Israel?" It's because the Jewish people's task in the history of salvation has two phases. The first was to birth God into the world. The second is to receive him the day he comes back!

The Messiah is coming, and when he comes back he will return to the Jewish people, to his land Israel and to the capital city, Jerusalem. The day is coming when the Messiah will restore the fallen tents of David. Not until then will the Jewish people come into their rest, and there will be many of us who will weep with them in thankfulness for the suffering that they have gone through on behalf of us all. ✡

# PART III

## The Anti-Semitic History Of The Church

# ט

# "All Of The Victims Were Jews, All Of The Murderers Christians"

IN OUR ORGANIZATION'S efforts to help the Jewish people, we have come face to face with the raw, naked evil of anti-Semitism many times. But perhaps the most surprising experience has been discovering the role of the church in the manhunt of the Jews that has gone on for nearly 2,000 years and that culminated during World War II. We have come to the realization and the nearly unfathomable conclusion that what Adolf Hitler did was nothing new. He merely took it upon himself to finish what the church had started nearly 2,000 years before: to solve the "Jewish problem" once and for all.

**A conversation with Moldavian Jews**
There are still thousands of Jews today in Kishinev, the capital city of Moldavia. There is also a Messianic church there. Through our

# PART III — THE ANTI-SEMITIC HISTORY OF THE CHURCH

work in Romania we have come in contact with this church and their evangelistic work. They have told us how difficult it is to talk to Jews in Moldavia about Jesus. The reason is that during the war, the Orthodox Church was on the side of the Nazis in their battle against the Jews of Europe. One woman's testimony in particular has etched itself on my mind forever. Her traumatic experience carries with it a message to all churches that want to spread the message of Jesus to our Jewish brothers and sisters.

When the Germans invaded Moldavia in the final phase of the war, a network was immediately set into place to find and deport the Moldavian Jews to a concentration camp in Eastern Europe. Of course the rumors had reached the Jews about the holocaust that was occurring, and one way for them to save their children was to give them away for adoption to childless Moldavian Christians. The woman we met had given away three of her children to a Christian couple who lovingly took care of them. Several months later she was arrested.

Before the Jews were deported to the concentration camp in Eastern Europe they were exhibited in the town squares. The whole ordeal was treated as a celebration, and the priests of the Orthodox Church, who actively participated in the Nazis' hunt for the Jews, were present. Eventually the German commander arrived and for a moment the jeers of the crowd quieted down. Some Jews were called forward, among them the woman who had given away her children. The commander asked many derogatory questions of the captured Jews and finally it was the woman's turn. He asked her what her name was, where she was from and finally if she had any children. The woman denied that she had any children and the commander repeated the question two more times. When she really insisted that she didn't have any children, the commander gave his soldiers a signal and after a moment a soldier came, bringing the woman's three children along with him! Somehow, maybe through a snitch, everything had been exposed.

"So, these aren't your children?" the commander asked cynically.

The woman said nothing.

"If these aren't your children," he continued, "then you won't mind if we kill them here and now!"

At that point the woman broke down completely. "They are my children!" she confessed. "But don't kill them. Take my life instead."

The commander asked the crowd, and along with the leaders of the church they shouted as one: "Kill the Jewish children!"

"But please, please take my life instead!" the mother pleaded.

"No," the commander said. "I want you to live with the death of your children seared upon your memory for the rest of your life."

The order was given and the children were executed there on the spot in the town square. The mother told us that they cut the children in pieces as the priests of the Orthodox Church ridiculed her, while all the people laughed and screamed, "Death to all Jews!"

There is an evil in man that runs so deep that our intellect cannot even fathom its depth. The Jewish people have been exposed to this evil for millennia. Too many times the Christian church has been both the source of and the fuel for these persecutions. This paradoxical conclusion is heartbreaking, but history has shown that the movement that Jesus founded, with the command to "love one another" and "turn the other cheek," can also be misused for perversion, where unfathomable evil is unleashed. It is therefore of utmost importance that Christians know their history. People who actively work with Israel and the Jews should especially know their own history. As a Christian, you cannot get close to the Jewish people in the same way that you get close to other groups.

## The church fathers laid the foundation for the anti-Semitism of our time

In the 100s a man named Melito, bishop of Sardis in minor Asia, was the first to formulate the myth about the murder of God: that the Jews killed Jesus. That whole line of thinking is incorrect since it was Rome's commander Pontius Pilate who passed the sentence and the Roman soldiers who carried it out. Theologically Jesus is "God

## PART III — THE ANTI-SEMITIC HISTORY OF THE CHURCH

come in the flesh"—and he couldn't be killed. We sing every Easter that "Jesus gave his life for the world." So how could the Jews kill him? This way of thinking has terrible consequences since, if Jesus was killed, then you remove the essence of the act of salvation, which builds upon the fact that Jesus, truly God and truly man, willingly gave up his life in exchange for all of fallen mankind.

In the 200s the legendary and theologically respected Greek church father Origen of Alexandria, in his commentary on the gospel of Matthew, did not see through this myth that even claimed that the church should take on the task of condemning and punishing the Jews. Quite the opposite, he was duped by this false teaching which would, throughout the centuries, devour large portions of the church from the inside. "Pilate washed his hands," Origen wrote, "but the Jews didn't want to be washed by the blood of Christ but rather let it come over them as revenge, since they said: 'May his blood be on us and on our children!'" (see Matt. 27:24–25). Origen interpreted this in such a way as to mean that it was the church's responsibility to demand revenge on the Jews. During the course of the centuries, hundreds of prominent thinkers among bishops and theologians have interpreted this text in the same way. Referring to Origen and his great authority, they have since acted the role of both the judge and the executioner on many occasions. Even though Jesus came to save and not to condemn (see John 3:17), the church has both condemned and implemented the punishment, and all of this has its basis in a theological lie.

By the second century the church leaders had started to purposefully suppress the Jewish background and nature of the New Testament, which resulted in declaring Jews to be heretics at a church meeting in Nice in 325. The myth and the lie of the murder of God made up the basis for this decision and the church took its first steps toward what would become the Jews' own walk down the Via Dolorosa. Replacement teaching was born, the theological school of thought that says that Israel has now been replaced by the church in its role in history. At the church meeting it was decided that whoever keeps the Sabbath, eats kosher, eats unleavened bread during Passover would be excommunicated from the church that the Jew Jesus founded. It is a mystery that such a decision could be arrived at, not least of all with the backdrop of what Paul really teaches, if you study all of his teaching. The Jews, Paul teaches, are the very root that holds up the rest of the tree. The Gentile Christians are a wild olive branch that has been grafted into the true tree. So Judaism, the covenant God made with Abraham and the Jews, is the foundation upon which Jesus could enter the world.

Confessing Jesus as Messiah means becoming a part of this foundation. Receiving life in Christ indirectly means that you cherish the role of the Jewish people in the history of what God is doing to bring salvation to man (see Romans 11:11–21). When the church cut off its ties to the Jews in the 300s, it committed—figuratively-speaking—suicide, since without a root, no living branches can emerge and be kept alive. That is also why large portions of the later church became an unkempt wild bush, growing in any way they pleased and having branches that withered continually. They wither since the church has cut itself off from access to the nourishment and divine genetic code that the Jewish people have enriched the church with.

The decision at the church meeting in Nice was probably the first official decision in which the church called the Jews heretics, but more were to come, and eventually a church-established set of regulations had emerged. It was a set of regulations that was strongly anti-Jewish in every way. Just read the three following canons from the Council in Laodicea in 364 A.D.: Canon number 29: "Christians must not judaize by resting on the Sabbath, but must work on that day; rather honoring the Lord's Day, and, if they can, resting then as Christians. But if any shall be found to be judaizers, let them be cut off from Christ." Canon number 37: "It is not lawful to receive portions sent from the feasts of Jews or heretics, nor to feast together with them." Canon number 38: "It is not lawful to receive unleavened bread from the Jews, nor to be partakers of their impiety."

# PART III — THE ANTI-SEMITIC HISTORY OF THE CHURCH

**John Chrysostom—worse than most**

In the aftermath of the church meeting in Nice, many anti-Semitic church leaders eventually emerged. One of the worst was John Chrysostom, who was a bishop and preacher in a town in present-day Syria from the years 386–397. In Antioch, many Christians had a friendly attitude toward Judaism. They gladly participated in the Jewish service on the Sabbath and on other holy days, went to Jewish doctors and often used Jewish courts. This was probably a result of the church that the first-generation Christians started in the city, a church where believing Jews and Gentiles held worship meetings together. It was here the believers were called Christians for the first time and it was from this church that Paul and Barnabas were called on a mission that would result in taking the gospel to Europe (see Acts 10–16).

So it is an irony of history that, in this same place where Gentiles and Jews blended together, where the Christian Jews generously opened their doors for the Gentiles who had come to faith and thus paved the way for the church of the Gentiles, head preacher John Chrysostom gave many anti-Semitic sermons 300 years later that would be spread widely throughout the Christian world. The following quote is an excerpt from one of these sermons:

"They sacrifice their sons and daughters to demons; they have insulted everything that is natural and nullified their own basic laws for human relations. They have become worse than wild animals and have without reason, with their own hands, murdered their own descendants in order to worship the vengeful demons that are enemies to our lives. They know only one thing, to satisfy their stomachs, become drunk, killing and beating each other. The Jews are the most worthless of all men. They are greedy, lustful and lazy. They are traitorous murderers of Christ. The Jews are the despicable murderers of Christ and for the crime of killing God there is absolutely no mercy or forgiveness. Christians shall never cease to demand revenge and the Jews must forever live in slavery. It is the duty of all Christians to hate the Jews."

*"All Of The Victims Were Jews, All Of The Murderers Christians"*

## From church father Augustine to the emperor Charlemagne
In the year 396 Augustine became bishop of the small coastal town of Hippo (in present-day Tunisia). He is often mentioned as one of the great fathers of the church. The difference between him and many others is that he did not want to kill the Jews, but wrote instead that "causing the humiliation of Jews everywhere would stand in contrast to the beauty of the church." In other words, they could serve as living proof of the lie of the synagogue and the truth of the church. This mindset is the same cynical way of thinking as the German commander we heard about in the beginning of this chapter—that Jews should only live so as to be made to suffer.

In the year 534 the famous Corpus Iuris Civilis was published, in which the emperor Justinian codified the Roman law. No other work in antiquity has had as much influence on the history of Europe. Under penalty of strict punishment, any sexual activity was forbidden between Jews and Christians. Jews that had an official office could no longer hold that position.

In the 600s many church meetings were held in which decisions were made concerning anti-Semitic measures. At a church meeting in 694 in Toledo, the capital city of Spain at the time, the bishops decided that when Jewish children turned seven, they were no longer allowed to live with their parents and could no longer have contact with them. The children were sent to nobles who would let them be raised by reliable Christians.

In the 800s the pressure seemed to decrease for a while. Charlemagne and those who followed him felt that Jews, who were knowledgeable and mastered many skills, were of great importance to international commerce. So the Jews got the right to life, free religious practice and possessions. They also got the freedom to participate in commerce, but paid an annual tenth of their income as a token of thanks for this protection. This Jew-friendly policy triggered the wrath of the Pope and the bishops and forced the emperor to change his attitude toward the Jews.

## The Crusades—"the horses waded in blood"
At the end of 1095 Pope Urban II urged a crusade to free Jerusalem from the hands of Islam. In the summer of 1096, when the crusade began, countless thousands of Jews were murdered in the region that is now called the Rhine, and their homes were plundered. "For why should we go into battle against the unfaithful in the Holy Land and leave the unfaithful in our midst at peace?" the crusaders asked. Even if the local bishop sometimes tried to stop the massacres, the chance to seize Jewish possessions without the threat of punishment was far too attractive. On the way down to the promised land, many Jewish societies were annihilated and a new wave of persecution spread across the world. It is said that when the crusaders took over Jerusalem—in the name of Jesus and with sword in hand—the Jews gathered together in the synagogue where they were burned alive. A testimony from one of the crusaders notes that the massacre was so complete that the horses waded in blood up to their knees.

In 1189 an extensive persecution broke out in the England of Richard the Lionheart, and in 1190 a great number of Jews were massacred in the English town of York. After that the Jews were driven from England. All of this occurred in the anti-Semitic spirit of the time that was continually supported by the church and its representatives.

In 1215 a regulation was put into effect by Pope Innocent and the bishops, by which Jews had to wear clothing different from that of the Christians so that Christians could avoid unknowingly having sexual contact with a Jew. Women who were guilty of racial mixture through sexual contact with Jews were dragged through the city on their way to the execution with a yellow hat on their heads. Many different regulations were put into place to clarify who was a Jew; for example a yellow mark or a yellow ring in France and a cone-shaped hat in Germany. These derogatory regulations could only be avoided if you got baptized. The yellow mark that was obligatory for Jews ever since the fourth Lateran Council preceded a different "solution to the Jewish problem." Jews were to be successively isolated and eliminated from society.

## The darkness and myths of the Middle Ages

During the Middle Ages the accusations against the Jews took on grotesque forms. During the early part of that epoch a myth originated that Jews ritually murdered Christian children. This myth, which has generated lots of misconceptions and suffering, developed over the course of several hundred years.

In the first stage of development it was claimed that the Jews murdered a Christian child during the week before Easter, preferably on Good Friday, in order to "crucify Jesus again." In the second stage of development it was claimed that Jews killed a child of Christian parents in connection with the celebration of Jewish Passover. It was claimed that Jews needed Christian blood to bake their unleavened bread and mix the bread with wine. But there was also a third version, one that sometimes appeared with the other two, sometimes on its own: that Jews needed Christian blood to do magic. The result of these accusations was that the church could fan the flame of hatred of the Jews and also justify the murder or expulsion of members of the Jewish population.

In the middle of the 1300s the Black Death broke out in Europe, which led to a third of the population dying in a short period of time. It was unknown how the disease spread, but soon rumors were going around that the Jews had poisoned the wells. So the plague was the work of the Jews. As a consequence, thousands of Jews were murdered in Basil, Strasbourg, Mainz, Worms and Cologne.

In 1215 Pope Innocent also introduced the theologically false teaching of transubstantiation. The transubstantiation teaching is confirmed by and canonized in the Catholic church, and signifies a change in the way the Eucharist—Communion—was seen. This new false teaching stated that Jesus was physically transubstantiated just before the Communion, so that the bread was transformed to Christ's real body and the wine to his blood.

This false teaching in its turn resulted in the myth that the Jews stole Communion flasks and stuck needles in them in order to crucify Jesus once again. This, in itself, is an illogical accusation, since

# PART III — THE ANTI-SEMITIC HISTORY OF THE CHURCH

it was the Roman soldiers who performed the execution. The result was yet another wave of persecution and massacres.

In Tyrol this myth was exploited and in some churches there were myths painted on the ceilings of how Jews committed ritual murders. These paintings are still preserved in several of Tyrol's churches today. The artist, Andered von Rim, was later made a saint by the Catholic church as a token of thanks for his anti-Semitic art.

During the second half of the Middle Ages, more and more vocational groups joined guilds. Only Christians were allowed to be members and only members were allowed to practice their handiwork. In that way the Jews were shut out of more and more job opportunities. The only thing that was allowed in the end—besides commerce with used items—was loaning out money for interest. This was forbidden for Christians since the church considered it to be a major sin. This development resulted in a new and persistent anti-Semitic, stereotypical myth: the Jew as a greedy usurer.

Between the 1100s and the 1400s southern Spain was set free once again from Islam. Forced baptisms took place everywhere, which even Jews had to suffer through. Baptized Jews who had converted to Christianity were ridiculed and called marranos (pigs) and suspected of secretly holding on to Judaism. As an answer to this "danger" the Spanish theologians invented a new teaching about the purity of the blood. According to this teaching, a baptized Jew was still a Jew and was therefore a danger to society in the eyes of the theologians. Even the converted Jews' great-grandchildren were persecuted. Extermination and expulsion were the only ways to save the Spanish population from "contagious" Jewish blood. During the Spanish Inquisition, launched during the latter half of the 1400s, King Ferdinand and Queen Isabella set up a court to purify the church from those who secretly held on to their Judaism. Mass arrests followed. In 1481 the first Jewish victims were burned at the stake. During the years that followed, about 30,000 Jews were murdered in this cruel way.

It might be appropriate here to describe how an execution took place. The Inquisition's grand public celebration was the auto-de-fé. This was an exhibition that gathered huge crowds of people, where the heretic was placed in front of a priest, who preached to the arrested victim with great enthusiasm. The highlight came after the sermon, when the heretics the priest had preached to were burned alive to the great delight of the crowd.

Since the Jews were blamed for doing everything they could to destroy Christianity, Ferdinand decided in 1492 to deport all of the Jews from Spain, which meant that 185,000 Jews were sent out of the country.

### The reformer Martin Luther—"free us from the Jews"

Martin Luther really did have an enlightened way of seeing things at the beginning of his ministry. He held a sound view of the Jews and he wanted to reform the Catholic Church, not to start a denomination. Martin Luther risked his life to help bring about one of the absolute biggest revivals in history. Through the power of God a new, vibrant church emerged. As always, this led to great benefits for the people.

Unfortunately, Luther changed over the years. He who had risked everything for the individual's right to the Word and belief in God was ensnared by Europe's governing bodies. That is why he wrote, at the end of his life in 1543, *Von den Juden und ihren Lügen* ("The Jews and Their Lies"). In it he outlines the following anti-Jewish policy: "First, to set fire to their synagogues and to bury and cover with dirt whatever will not burn." He lists a seven-step plan of action that the German Nazis would put into effect four hundred years later:

1. Burn their synagogues.
2. Destroy their homes.
3. Destroy their Scriptures.
4. Forbid rabbis completely.
5. Put them in ghettos.
6. Seize their possessions.
7. Put them in work camps.

# PART III — THE ANTI-SEMITIC HISTORY OF THE CHURCH

During the 1500s, 1600s, and 1700s, the church divided into three large units—the Catholic church, the Orthodox Church and the Protestant church. All of them continued their Jew-hating policies. From the pulpits in northern Europe, the czar's Russia and the Pope's Italy, new fuel was constantly added to the fire that eventually would become an excellent tool in the hand of Adolf Hitler. What the church had been desperate to do for 2,000 years, he would make happen: extermination of the Jews.

## The racial teaching of the 1800s and the anti-Semitism of the church are intertwined

In the middle of the 1800s a new concept called "racial theory" arose. It was claimed that the battle between the races was the key to understanding world history. People are not good or bad by coincidence but based on their belonging to a certain race. Some people even claimed that only the purely "Aryan" (Caucasian or Germanic) race possesses truly high culture. It was claimed that the Jews belonged to a special race, called "Semitic," whose purpose was to undermine and destroy the Aryan race. In this way Jews and Judaism were no longer condemned on religious grounds but on prescribed scientific grounds.

At the end of the 1800s *The Protocols of the Learned Elders of Zion* was published in Russia, a fabricated report from what was said to be a secret meeting of rabbis. This report claimed that the Jews had sworn on oath to take over the whole world. The book unifies old Christian anti-Jewish prejudices with the new anti-Semitism that is based on racial teaching.

The Russian Orthodox Church played a big role in the preservation of extremely anti-Jewish views for many centuries. The church identified itself completely with the so-called Holy Russia. Just the presence of the Jews brought dishonor to this holy Russia, and the Jews should therefore be expelled. The Russian authorities tried to put the blame for their social and economic difficulties on the Jews, especially after a group of Russian revolutionaries murdered Alexan-

## "All Of The Victims Were Jews, All Of The Murderers Christians"

der II in 1881. In the 1880s many pogroms took place in the Ukraine. In Kiev, Russian soldiers stood and watched while Jewish homes and businesses were plundered. In 1891 all Jews were deported from Moscow. After Russia's defeat to Japan in 1905, an event that had been considered unthinkable, anti-Jewish violence increased even more.

Racial teaching and the anti-Semitism of the church eventually became intertwined. Adolf Stöcker, head preacher in Berlin, summarized the attitudes that preceded the Holocaust in the following sermon: "But I am thrilled since here in Berlin we have begun to put a stop to Jewish dominance in society. The Jews are guilty of the utmost irritation of all of the peoples of the world. The anti-Semitic movement is sweeping across the entire earth. Gentlemen, everywhere that the Jews' dominance can no longer be put up with, the people are arising to cast off the yoke. We declare war on the Jews to defeat them at their very foundation, and we will not rest until they have fallen from the pedestal on which they stood here in Berlin and land in the dust, where they belong."

### The final solution—an act of Nazism or the culmination of the fallen church's Jewish persecution?

Hitler's anti-Semitism was influenced by Luther's anti-Semitic writings. In March of 1924, Hoheneichen-Verlag in Munich published an unfinished manuscript by Hitler's friend Dietrich Eckart. From this work, *Gespräche mit Hitler* ("Conversations with Hitler"), it is clearly seen that Hitler was well informed about the development of the church's anti-Jewish doctrine and policy during the previous centuries.

Hitler knew that Luther, during the breakthrough years of the reformation, had a friendly attitude toward the Jews. But when Luther later wrote his book *Von den Juden und ihren Lügen* ("The Jews and Their Lies") he had, according to Hitler, realized his mistake. Not until the end of his life did Luther see the Jews in the same way that the people of the 1900s saw them: fully exposed, as a warning for all people and all times. If Luther had realized it earlier, then the Jews would have disappeared from government and aristocracy when Luther was still young. Finally Hitler pointed out that Luther advised the princes to set fire to the synagogues and Jewish schools. But Hitler could not see that it would have done any good. Even if there had no longer been any synagogues or Jewish schools, the Jewish spirit would still have existed and exercised its influence. There isn't a Jew, one single Jew, that doesn't incarnate that spirit, he said.

"If it really is so, that every Jew in Europe incarnates that evil, devilish spirit, then it isn't enough to set fire to synagogues and Jewish schools, but all Jews must be exterminated," Hitler later wrote in *Mein Kampf.*

But Hitler was also influenced by the Catholic church's anti-Jewish teachings and practices. Hitler's friend Hans Frank wrote that Hitler told him in 1938 that two bishops visited him (Hitler) on April 26, 1933, as representatives for the German bishops' meeting. "They attacked me for my way of treating the Jews. For fifteen centuries the Catholic church has considered Jews to be parasites and sent them to the ghetto. They knew what Jews were. I am just continuing with what has occurred for fifteen centuries. Maybe in that way I am doing Christianity a great service."

To Pastor Berning in 1933 he said: "What is it you really have against my way of treating the Jews? I have just been consistent. I am doing what the Catholic church has done for fifteen centuries. The difference between the church and me is that I get the job done."

"There is no innocent blood in Jewish children anywhere in the entire world!"

The rabbi W.M.D. Weismandel writes in his memoirs about his and Rabbi Nietra's experiences in Slovakia during World War II. In 1942, Rabbi Nietra turned to Archbishop Kametko to ask him to help stop Jews from being deported. The rabbi pointed out the risk of starvation and disease that the women, elderly and innocent children would be exposed to. At that point the rabbi had still not found out about the gas chambers.

The archbishop answered: "This isn't about deportation. You aren't going to die of starvation and misery. They are going to murder you all, old and young, women and children, at once—that is the punishment you deserve for murdering our Lord and Savior, Jesus Christ. There is only one possibility of avoiding this fate: convert to our religion and I will do my best to get the decision revoked."

In 1944, Weismandel himself was deported with his entire family to a transition camp, and from there to Auschwitz. When he succeeded in escaping, he went immediately to the ambassador to the pope* to tell him about the terrible conditions in which thousands of children were forced to live in the concentration camp. The pope's ambassador wanted to get rid of him as soon as possible and said: "It is Sunday today, a holy day for us. Tiss [the governing leader] and I don't concern ourselves with worldly matters on such a holy day."

Weismandel replied, wondering how the blood of innocent children could be counted as a "worldly matter," and the ambassador said: "There is no innocent blood in Jewish children anywhere in the world. All Jewish blood is guilty. You have to die. That is the punishment that awaits for your sin."

## "While all of the victims were Jews, all of the murderers were Christians"

Before we make some conclusions from this chapter, let me now quote Nobel Prize winner Elie Wiesel.

"It takes us back to the beginning: the relationship between Jews and Christians. In this chaos we should look at their relationship in a new light. Because a new truth has hit us: while all of the victims were Jews, all of the murderers were Christians. How can you explain that the Pope never excommunicated Hitler or Himmler? That Pius XII never felt that it was important, or even necessary, to condemn Auschwitz? That in the SS there were many Christians who held on to their Christian traditions even to the end? That some murderers went to confession between murders? And that all of them came from Christian homes and had received a Christian upbringing? How can you explain that their Christian faith didn't cause their hands to shake when they shot a child to death, or that their consciences didn't revolt when they brought naked and abused victims into the death factories?"

**Truth and consequence**
It has been incredibly painful for me to write this chapter, partly because of the sufferings the Jews have been exposed to but also because the persecutions have come through the Christian church. The unavoidable truth is that the Nazis were certainly those who wielded the axe of the executioner, but that axe was forged by the anti-Semitic doctrines that the church and the western world developed for nearly 2,000 years. The Nazis didn't come up with something new—they picked up on and then carried out 2,000 years of anti-Semitic church history. "The final solution," Hitler said. The solution to the church's problem with the Jews? The truth is that we were all present when the Jewish people were being exterminated. Europe knew what was happening, but everyone kept silent when the Jews were gassed to death!

The anti-Semitic focus of Nazism was founded when the church fathers, one hundred years after Jesus' death and resurrection, came up with the lie about the murder of God. This lie did not only kill the Jews but also the church itself. The doctrine that God "gave his one and only Son" and that his death on the cross was an exchange where God took the place of sinful man was instead exchanged for the lie that the Jews killed Jesus. But you cannot kill God! The consequence of this lie, and the consequence of shutting out Jews from the church that the Jew Jesus and his Jewish apostles founded, was that the church lost its way. Within a few centuries the Christian faith got all mixed up with pagan Roman religions. By the 500s a syncretic religion had emerged that called itself the Catholic church. Out of this religious mixture an empire had been built with the Pope himself as the leader. Now the following were implemented: pagan celebrations, belief in purgatory, penance, believing that the Lord's communion is a sacrifice that can only be administered by priests, division of the church into men of office and laymen, worship of martyrs and relics, celibacy, the worship of Mary, letters of indulgence, religious war, etc. The rhetorical question is: If the Jewish Christians had been a part of the emerging church, would purgatory, relics, and worship of Mary have even been possible in the church? The answer is no. Could the church have lost its way in such a manner if the Jewish Christians had had the chance to make up the foundation (root) of the church, as they are called to be? Again, the answer is no.

Now someone might ask: "But how can you belong to a church that has laid the very foundation for the Holocaust, and that has gone to war and committed bestial acts in the name of the church?"

The answer is that I don't belong to that church. My conviction is that there is another church, one that has always existed, and it is that church to which I belong. It hasn't written history; the institutionalized and political church has done that. The false, syncretic "church" has persecuted two groups throughout its history: the Jews and the "revival Christians." Just like the Jews, the revival church has been deported from place to place. Often the Jews and the revival Christians have been burnt at the same stake.

How can you know which church is which? The Jewish issue is one of great dividers. We can see it clearly today. The church movements that are growing right now are doing so through people who selflessly sacrifice themselves so that other people can encounter the atonement found in Christ. These churches, if they have sound Biblical teaching, have insight into the Jewish people's special place in God. I know because I have met and taught such people from all over the world. The interesting thing is that even Muslims from the Middle East, with an anti-Semitic political past, are able to see the big picture of God's plan with the Jewish people when they finally meet and get to know the true, living Jesus. This church doesn't evangelize with a sword in hand but rather with love as a weapon. This church is ready to give their own lives so as to save others. Such a church is wonderful to experience.

That is why we must tell the truth about the fallen church's anti-

# PART III — THE ANTI-SEMITIC HISTORY OF THE CHURCH

Semitic history. It is partly for our own (the church's) survival. The Jews, and the covenant that God made with them, are the root from which the whole tree gets its sustenance. Into this tree, Paul teaches, the Gentile Christians have been grafted. And he warns the church about boasting over the root when he writes that "it is not you who support the root but the root [read 'the Jews'] that supports you" (see Rom. 11:16–19).

The church that distances itself from God's covenant with the Jews cuts itself off from the root and the life that root gives. The church that killed itself in the 300s by denouncing the Jews as heretics has at times—in theory and in practice—shown itself to be an anti-Christian church. Its actions reveal its very essence! It progressively withers, yet keeps itself "alive" through political power and control. But since the time of the ancient church there has always been another church that has protected the Jewish people and the true gospel.

It is incredibly important to know church history in order to be able to draw close to the Jews in the correct way. I believe in Jesus. I know that he is the Messiah. I also know that we are to preach the gospel to all people. But with the true historical context as a background, I realize that the only way I can draw close to the Jewish people is to draw close to them in the way Jesus drew close to me: with unlimited, selfless love. ✡

# PART IV

## The End Times

## Scattered To The Ends Of The Earth

IN THE 50s AND 60s A.D. the innermost core of the Roman Empire suffered through many trials and catastrophes. Famine, plague, earthquakes and internal power struggles caused the influence of Rome over its occupied regions to weaken. One of the most oppressed of the occupied lands was Israel. The Romans took their money and ridiculed them for their monotheistic faith. After Caesar Augustus was given the status of a god, sacrifices were made to him in the entire Roman kingdom and he was worshipped. Of course this was of enormous significance in Israel. There was an increase in the expectation that the Messiah would come and make Israel a great power again, and many different resistance movements emerged in the land.

When Rome experienced the catastrophic fire of 64 A.D., things started to happen very quickly. The spark that ignited this chain of events was the battle over a piece of land in Israel—a situation that we can recognize even today. Rome was for the moment in a weakened state, and the different Jewish resistance movements that had waited decades for this opportunity reacted with haste. The freeing of Jerusalem went surprisingly easy, the daily, abominable sacrifice to Caesar was done away with and the revolt against Rome spread quickly across the whole land.

But despite the political unrest in Rome, the Roman leaders acted with authority and appointed the highly merited military commander Vespasian with the task of suppressing the Jewish revolt. He brought along his young son Titus to help him. With three legions, a total of 50,000 soldiers, they marched toward Israel. The war began in 66. Vespasian tactically destroyed city after city as a means of cutting off and isolating Jerusalem. In 68 the emperor Nero died and a new power struggle erupted in Rome. The evil march came to a stop for about a year. In 70 A.D., Vespasian was proclaimed emperor of Rome. He left Israel and handed down the mission of marching toward Jerusalem to his son Titus.

Jerusalem, which had been cut off from its surroundings for nearly two years, was struggling with internal battles. Even though they were confronting such a superior enemy as Rome, the Jews still could not succeed in uniting their forces; instead, there was a civil war going on inside the walls of Jerusalem even during the siege itself. It was toward this Jerusalem—where about a million Jews were now gathered—that the new commander Titus marched. It was a Jerusalem plagued by famine and internal strife, but still they held onto a fanatic belief that they could defeat Rome.

Titus had camped in Jericho. Now he marched on the frontline with his forces on the legendary road between Jericho and Jerusalem. A few kilometers before he arrived, he ordered his troops to a halt. From a distance he saw the city that is "a cup of drunkenness to all surrounding peoples," and he was astonished with admiration. The golden temple rose majestically over Jerusalem and reached toward the cloudless sky. Titus was overwhelmed. He had never seen anything more beautiful. He gave the order to keep the temple intact when they invaded Jerusalem. But that order stood in contradiction to all of the prophecies about the fall of Jerusalem that had been uttered throughout the centuries, and which were finally summarized by Jesus himself:

> *For days will come upon you when your enemies will build an embankment around you, surround you and close you in on every side, and level you, and your children within you, to the ground; and they will not leave in you one stone upon another, because you did not know the time of your visitation.* Luke 19:43–44

When the legions of Rome, after nearly two years of siege, broke through the Jewish lines of defense in 70 A.D., these prophecies went into fulfillment. The Jewish defenders set fire to the embankments as a means of defense. But soon the fire got out of control and spread quickly across the temple area. There were gold-embellished cedarwood panels everywhere. Finally the fire reached the temple itself. All of the gold melted and ran down between the white stone blocks that formed the foundation that the entire temple area rested upon. When the battle was over and the conquering soldiers plundered the city, they started tearing down the temple, despite the orders Titus had given. Stone by stone, the temple was demolished so that the plunderers could gain access to the gold that had run down in between the joints of the white stone blocks. When the plundering was over and the last of the Jews had been executed, the glorious Jerusalem that Titus had wanted to preserve now lay in ruins. Since that day, Jesus' prophecy has echoed throughout the centuries that "they will not leave in you one stone upon another."

Hundreds of thousands of Jews lost their lives in this war. The massacre was massive. The ones who survived were sent to the amphitheaters in the big cities to be sacrificed in the bloody gladiator games. There were less than 100,000 Jews left.

Sixty years later Simon bar Kochba proclaimed himself as messiah to a nearly obliterated Israel. The small remnant of people that was left rose up once again against the empire of Rome. The result was devastating. Rome decided to exterminate the Jewish population in Israel completely. Nearly one thousand villages and communities were destroyed and leveled, the entire land was deserted, and a Roman city called Aelia Capitolina was built upon the ruins of Jerusalem. The surviving Jews were forced to leave their land and the Romans gave the land a new name instead: Palestine. The name was an insult to the Jews, and it denoted a group of people that didn't even exist anymore, but who had once been the Jews' archenemy, the Philistines.

**Forced to move from place to place**
Now commenced a period in the history of the Jewish people when they were forced to move from place to place. The blessing that the Jewish people had sometimes experienced in the promised land was now replaced with the exact opposite. They barely had time to settle before lies and slander provoked new pogroms. If the Jews didn't flee of their own accord, the authorities forced them out.

Many prophecies in the Bible describe with incredible accuracy the future suffering the Jewish people would have to go through. One of the strongest prophetic portrayals is spoken by Moses:

> *You shall be plucked from off the land which you go to possess. Then the LORD will scatter you among all peoples, from one end of the earth to the other, and there you shall serve other gods, which neither you nor your fathers have known—wood and stone. And among those nations you shall find no rest, nor shall the sole of your foot have a resting place; but there the LORD will give you a trembling heart, failing eyes, and anguish of soul. Your life shall hang in doubt before you; you shall fear day and night, and have no assurance of life. In the morning you shall say, 'Oh, that it were evening!' And at evening you shall say, 'Oh, that it were morning!' because of the fear which*

*terrifies your heart, and because of the sight which your eyes see.* Deuteronomy 28:63b–67

With the history of the Jewish people as proof, it is hard to dispute the statements made in this prophecy. "No rest … despair … never sure of your life." The Jewish people are loved by God, but still he did not and does not withhold the consequences that would come upon them if they turn their backs on him. The hand of God can be seen even in the incredible suffering that the Jewish people have gone through. Jesus foretold that:

*And they will fall by the edge of the sword, and be led away captive into all nations. And Jerusalem will be trampled by Gentiles until the times of the Gentiles are fulfilled.* Luke 21:24

But Jerusalem would not be in the hand of the Gentiles forever, but one day in the future Jerusalem would again reign as the city of the Jewish people.

## To the ends of the earth

There is yet another prophecy that reappears among many of the Bible's prophets. It is the prophecy that the Jewish people will be driven to the ends of the earth, to all the nations, to the four corners of the earth. Moses writes this:

*Then the LORD will scatter you among all peoples, from one end of the earth to the other, and there you shall serve other gods, which neither you nor your fathers have known—wood and stone.* Deuteronomy 28:64

The first phase involved the scattering of the Jewish people among all peoples, from one end of the earth to the other. When this had happened the next phase would begin, when the Jewish people would be gathered again to Israel:

## PART IV — THE END TIMES

*Therefore say, "Thus says the Lord GOD: 'I will gather you from the peoples, assemble you from the countries where you have been scattered, and I will give you the land of Israel.'"* Ezekiel 11:17

If you weave the history of the Jewish people into these Bible verses, you can see that the actual events have matched the predictions of the Bible in a remarkable way. When the Jews were forced to flee the land after the destruction of Jerusalem and the Bar Kochba rebellion, a geographic scattering ensued. The Jewish people were forced to move from place to place. First they moved to the region around the eastern Mediterranean, but when the church became more and more anti-Semitic in the 300s, many Jews moved on. Many of them ended up all the way up in England after the passing of a few centuries. In Mesopotamia the same thing occurred when Islam emerged in the 600s. Many Jews were forced further east as Islam conquered parts of Asia. In Europe in the 1500s, just when there were no countries left to migrate to, the door to a new continent was opened: America. So by the time history reached the 1800s, the prophecies had been fulfilled; there were Jews scattered from one end of the earth to the other.

It says that Abraham "believed" in the promises he received from God. But it was impossible for him to see the extent of what God was calling him and his people to. Countries and continents he wasn't even aware of would be populated by his descendants, the Jews. Everywhere their unshakable faith in the one and only God would be a testimony to everyone of the covenant between God and the Jews. Just think that after four thousand years, the calling that started with Abraham in the tiny Mesopotamian city of Ur would leave its mark from one end of the earth to the other. ✡

## The Return — From The Four Corners Of The Earth

WHEN YOU STUDY THE BIBLE you discover after a while that the prophecies have a life of their own. Prophetic utterances that have been incomprehensible for ages suddenly prove to be quite relevant to the present time. It is as though the prophecies that were spoken long ago are lying in wait throughout the epochs of history, ready to be activated when the time is right, activated to implement God's plans and purposes. Isaiah writes:

> "For My thoughts are not your thoughts, nor are your ways My ways," says the LORD. "For as the heavens are higher than the earth, so are My ways higher than your ways, and My thoughts than your thoughts. For as the rain comes down, and the snow from heaven, and do not return there, but water the earth, and make it bring forth and bud, that it may give seed to the sower and bread to the eater, so shall My word be that goes forth from My mouth; it shall not return to the void, but it shall accomplish

*what I please, and it shall prosper in the thing for which I sent it."* Isaiah 55:8–11

The Lord's thoughts are not like man's thoughts. The difference is enormous. God the Almighty, All-knowing, Omnipresent and Eternal knows and sees everything and can do everything. "Have you ever seen a raindrop stop three feet above the ground and return to the sky?" God seems to ask Isaiah. "You haven't? It's the same way with the prophecies that I have spoken to you. The words carry within themselves an inner power, so that they won't return to me until they have accomplished what I sent them to accomplish."

**Prophecies activated after 2,500 years**
As time went by, history unfolded. The Jews moved from land to land. But all over the world, wherever they settled, the Jewish people never forgot Jerusalem. They mentioned Jerusalem daily in their prayers, constantly reminded of the Bible's 700 promises that they would one day return to the land of promise Israel. Every Passover the promise was repeated: "Next year in Jerusalem!" But despite all of the promises, I don't think that the first Jews who reached Argentina or the southern part of South America thought: "This must be one of the four corners of the earth, now we can't go any farther. This must mean that we can finally return to Israel." Nor did the Jewish families who moved to Alaska during the days of the gold rush, or who fled to eastern Siberia for anti-Semitic reasons, think that way. The idea of "next year in Jerusalem" had become an unfulfillable dream that they stubbornly held onto. But the strange thing is that around the same time that the Jewish people reached the four corners of the earth, bold and daring ideas were birthed among some scattered Jewish groups in Russia that they barely dared to imagine anymore: the dream of truly returning to Israel, to Zion.

For more than 2,500 years, words that had been spoken by Israel's prophets had lain dormant, waiting to get activated. But sometime in the 1800s, without forewarning and when the world least realized it, these words of God began to get activated. Once again the Jews in the worldwide dispersion began to dream of returning to the land of their fathers. Some of them breathed life into that dream, and within a few decades it was no longer a dream, but rather a reality of what had been predestined, though hidden, for thousands of years.

*The word that came to Jeremiah from the LORD, saying, "Thus speaks the LORD God of Israel, saying: 'Write in a book for yourself all the words that I have spoken to you. For behold, the days are coming,' says the LORD, 'that I will bring back from captivity My people Israel and Judah,' says the LORD. 'And I will cause them to return to the land that I gave to their fathers, and they shall possess it.'"* Jeremiah 30:1-3

## Bold ideas are birthed among the Russian Jews

In Russia, the Russian Orthodox Church played a large role in maintaining extreme anti-Jewish views. The church identified itself completely with holy Russia, and since the mere presence of Jews would dishonor holy Russia, they were not allowed to settle there. The authorities in their turn did their part to try to place the blame for social and economic difficulties on the Jews, especially since a group of Russian revolutionaries murdered Alexander II in 1881. Many of the minor rights that the Jews had up to that time were done away with completely. In the 1880s many pogroms took place in the Ukraine. In 1891 all of the Jews were forced to leave Moscow.

It was in this environment and among these Russian Jews that the bold idea of returning to Zion—Jerusalem—first emerged. A generation of pioneers had grown up in Russia, ready to give up everything to return to Israel. From the middle of the 1800s until World War I, five waves of Jewish settlers came to Israel, approximately 70,000, mostly from Russia and Eastern Europe. They all had an unwavering determination to build up the land again; a land that had lay desert and withering for 2,000 years. David Melchior wrote: "It wouldn't be wrong to say that Palestine (Israel) has not been a country for nearly

2,000 years, but rather something in between a desert with scattered ruins and a burial ground." Mark Twain made the same observance when he said: "The promised land has lost its glory." Ever since the 300s the land had been left to its fate, and the curse that Moses had uttered had been resting upon it:

> *The coming generation of your children who rise up after you, and the foreigner who comes from a far land, would say, when they see the plagues of that land and the sicknesses which the LORD has laid on it: "The whole land is brimstone, salt, and burning; it is not sown, nor does it bear, nor does any grass grow there ..."* Deuteronomy 29:22

## And the desert began to blossom

Before World War I the land was a part of the Ottoman kingdom and was owned by Egyptian and Turkish merchants. The lowlands by the coast in Galilee and the Jezreel valley had turned into swamplands where malaria was rampant. It was sulfur and salt; the earth was completely torched. But the land would not remain a wilderness:

> *When all these things come upon you, the blessing and the curse which I have set before you, and you call them to mind among all the nations where the LORD your God drives you, and you return to the LORD your God and obey His voice, according to all that I command you today, you and your children, with all your heart and with all your soul, that the LORD your God will bring you back from captivity, and have compassion on you, and gather you again from all the nations where the LORD your God has scattered you. If any of you are driven out to the farthest parts under heaven, from there the LORD your God will gather you, and from there He will bring you. Then the LORD your God will bring you to the land which your fathers possessed, and you shall possess it. He will prosper you and multiply you more than your fathers. The LORD your God will make you abound in all*

*the work of your hand, in the fruit of your body, in the increase of your livestock, and in the produce of your land for good. For the LORD will again rejoice over you for good as He rejoiced over your fathers.* Deuteronomy 30:1–5, 9

The Jewish Zionists risked their lives to cultivate the land of Israel. Meir Karchevsky, who had experienced the pogroms in Russia at the beginning of the 1880s, was among the first to immigrate to Israel. In 1881 he came to Jaffa, where he placed his family in a simple inn while he went out to find property. In 1882 he and a few others bought a piece of property ten kilometers outside of Jaffa. They called the place Rishon Le-Zion, which means "the first in Zion." Now the prophetic hour had come. Slowly but surely the withered land began to awaken to life. It was as though the land sensed that the Jewish people had entered her, and the lifeblood of the land started to pulsate as more and more Jews returned to Israel. The desert began to blossom and the parched land turned into lush fields. It was as though the essence of the land itself was preparing to be born again, to become a mother to the people that would pour into it from the four corners of the earth after the end of World War II. *"The wilderness and the wasteland shall be glad for them, and the desert shall rejoice and blossom as the rose"* (Is 35:1).

### They were both from Vienna

It is strange to consider that around the turn of the century two men, almost at the same time, were walking the streets of Vienna. One was Adolf Hitler, who would later personify evil itself as he put his hate for the Jews into action. But there was also another man in Vienna, a Jewish journalist named Theodor Herzl. Herzl was a secularized Jew who received an assignment from his newspaper, *Neue Freie Presse*, to report on the trial in Paris against a French officer named Dreyfus, a Jew. The trial against Dreyfus was a miscarriage of justice—he was blamed for high treason against the French state that someone else had committed.

## PART IV — THE END TIMES

Herzl was present when the verdict was given and when the officer Dreyfus was demoted in humiliation. During his days in Paris, Herzl also witnessed firsthand the anti-Semitic atmosphere on the streets of Paris as mobs cried out, "Death to Dreyfus, death to the Jewish dogs."

Herzl restlessly wandered the streets of Paris at night and his Jewish heritage awakened on the inside of him. He realized that he had a responsibility and from that moment on his life was changed. In despair he returned to Vienna and a few months later had written the book that would become the manifest of Zionism, *Der Judenstaat* ("The Jewish State"). The book became a trumpet call for Zionism and on August 29, 1897, 204 delegates from seventeen countries met together. The meeting place was the concert hall in a huge casino in Basel, Switzerland. It was decided at this congress that they would: work to help farmers, craftsmen and businessmen immigrate to Israel; organize all of the Jews who were already in Israel; develop a registry of all of the Jews who had returned to Israel, and also make sure that they really were Jews; and prepare letters for relevant countries in order to influence them to work toward the goals of Zionism.

This was the starting point for all the political efforts whose goal was to establish a "Jewish state." On the final day of the congress Herzl jotted down the following prophetic words in his diary: "Were I to sum up the Basel Congress in a word—which I shall guard against pronouncing publicly—it would be this: At Basel I founded the Jewish State. If I said this out loud today l would be greeted by universal laughter. In five years perhaps, and certainly in fifty years, everyone will perceive it."

**A 100 percent Jewish national state is reduced to 15 percent**
So the first miracle of many took place. The government of Great Britain, on the initiative of the British royal house, gave Lord Arthur James Balfour the task of researching the possibility of giving the Jewish people a national home, their own land. Of course this assignment had been preceded by intense lobbying, but we also have

to see God's hand in this event: World War I ended in 1918 and the dominance of the Ottoman kingdom in the Middle East came to an end. The victors, including Great Britain, had conquered the area that was later given the name Palestine again. The famous General Allenby had invaded Jerusalem and because of the instability and chaos there, Great Britain was given responsibility for Jerusalem and the land around it in 1922. For a few years there was a political vacuum in the region.

In 1917 the Zionistic lobbyist groups finally got what they had been longing for when Lord Balfour established the famous Balfour declaration, calling for the establishment of a Jewish national home in Palestine. The entire country, meaning both sides of the river Jordan, were given to the Jewish people. It is remarkable that the borders that were drawn up in 1917 were almost identical to the borders the land was given when Joshua divided it up among the twelve tribes!

But in 1922 the political winds changed when oil came into the picture. The Arabs, who reacted violently against the Jewish people getting their own land from territory that they considered to be their own, used the newly discovered oilfields to put pressure on Great Britain. In one swift movement the Palestine mandate was redivided and 77 percent was given to the Arabic Bedouin tribes, the Hashemites! That 77 percent of land received the name Transjordan, which in the Bible was the regions of land that were given to Gad, Reuben and Manassah. But the Arabs didn't stop there; they also demanded the remaining 23 percent, all while Great Britain was growing more and more negative toward the increasing Jewish immigration to the region. The rapidly growing oil industry was more important to British politicians than the restoration of the Jewish people.

After the end of World War II, Jewish immigration escalated even though Arab hatred toward all of the Jews in the region grew more and more intense. With the Brits calling the shots, the United Nations stepped in and divided the remaining 23 percent yet again. Basically, all of Judea, Samaria and parts of Galilee were given to the Arabs. Of the land that was promised to the Jews in 1917, there was only 15 percent left! But nothing could stop God from bringing his people back home to Israel.

## Shall a nation be born at once?

*Therefore say, "Thus says the Lord GOD: 'I will gather you from the peoples, assemble you from the countries where you have been scattered, and I will give you the land of Israel.'"* Ezekiel 11:17

In 1942 the German chancellor Adolf Hitler revealed his intentions for the Jewish people. He had the final solution to the Jewish problem. The solution was total extermination of every Jew. Possessed by an evil that no words can describe, he evilly used a political strategy, a war machine and an infrastructure to efficiently execute six million Jews in five years. It's worth considering whether the true reason for the war might really have been to annihilate the Jews. There is the possibility that the war was just a cover. There was a spiritual dimension to all of it, and the key component was the Jewish people and their right to return to Israel. The battle between Moses and Pharaoh was played out again, but the difference this time was that the price was higher. The historic scenario remains as a witness to how Jews, who for 2,000 years had lived in exile, gained a foothold in the land during the 1800s; how Great Britain, through a unique historical exception, put it in writing to establish a Jewish national state in Israel. This was a Jewish political victory that in just a few decades turned into the greatest tragedy ever, the Holocaust. But even though Europe, with Great Britain at the forefront, forbid Jewish immigration to Israel in 1939, even though Hitler annihilated six million Jews during World War II, even though the pogroms continued right after World War II, even though many of the surviving Jews who headed to Israel were placed in British concentration camps in Cyprus, and even though 400 million Arabs declared war on this remnant of people, nobody could stop Herzl's prophetic words from 1897 from being fulfilled: "Not in five years, but in fifty years." On

## The Return — From The Four Corners Of The Earth

May 14, 1968, about fifty years after Herzl's statement, David Ben Gurion declared the establishment of the Jewish state of Israel!

*Who has heard such a thing? Who has seen such things? Shall the earth be made to give birth in one day? Or shall a nation be born at once? For as soon as Zion was in labor, She gave birth to her children.* Isaiah 66:8

## Through water and fire

*But now, thus says the LORD, who created you, O Jacob, and He who formed you, O Israel: "Fear not, for I have redeemed you; I have called you by your name; you are Mine. When you pass through the waters, I will be with you; and through the rivers, they shall not overflow you. When you walk through the fire, you shall not be burned, nor shall the flame scorch you. For I am the LORD your God, the Holy One of Israel, your Savior; I gave Egypt for your ransom, Ethiopia and Seba in your place. Since you were precious in My sight, you have been honored, and I have loved you; therefore I will give men for you, and people for your life. Fear not, for I am with you; I will bring your descendants from the east, and gather you from the west; I will say to the north, 'Give them up!' and to the south, 'Do not keep them back!' Bring My sons from afar, and My daughters from the ends of the earth—everyone who is called by My name, whom I have created for My glory; I have formed him, yes, I have made him."* Isaiah 43:1–7

Through water and fire—for 2,000 years! They had survived the wars of Rome, the massacres of the Crusaders, the Spanish inquisition and had even survived "the final solution." Even if their moral decay had at times been substantial, the Jews had still maintained the very foundation of Judaism: belief in the God of Abraham, Isaac and Jacob. Belief that they were and are a chosen people. Belief that the covenant that Abraham made with God and the collective covenant their ancestors had once made at the foot of Mt. Sinai would prove to be more powerful than any of their trials. The price was high, but anti-Semitism failed and the Jews conquered. Now they were back in the land of promise and would never be removed! "I will plant them in their own land, and no longer shall they be pulled up from the land I have given them," says the Lord your God (Amos 9:15). From east and west the Jewish people came, from the four corners of the earth, from the ends of the world. If they couldn't get there on their own, the Israeli military implemented risky rescue operations. The Arab states tried to eliminate the state of Israel many times, but despite their fully superior strength they always lost the wars against Israel.

However, to the north, hundreds of thousands of Jews were still waiting to be able to return to Israel. In the 1980s the former Soviet was so severely shaken that it collapsed, and the lands to the north could no longer hold back the Jewish people. Both Isaiah and Ezekiel had prophesied of a time when large masses of Jews would return from the north. Ezekiel probably questioned himself once or twice when he prophesied about a future miracle, a mass movement of people so great that it could be compared to the exodus from Egypt under Moses' leadership.

But today hundreds of thousands of Jews remind their children in Israel about the seventy-year imprisonment (1917-1987) in the former Soviet Union. They remind them so that they never forget that it was the hand of the Lord that made it possible for them to travel to Israel, far away from the oppression of totalitarian, communist, imperialist anti-Semitism. They will never forget the prayers they prayed to the God of their fathers that the Soviet borders would open, and how it all happened so quickly. In ten years' time (the 1990s), nearly one million Jews left the collapsed Soviet empire.

*Then say to them, "Thus says the Lord GOD: 'Surely I will take the children of Israel from among the nations, wherever they have gone, and will gather them from every side and bring them into their own land; and I will make them one nation in the land, on the mountains of Israel; and one king shall be king over them all; they shall no longer be two nations, nor shall they ever be divided into two kingdoms again.'"* Ezekiel 37:21-22

*"Therefore behold, the days are coming," says the LORD, "that it shall no more be said, 'The LORD lives who brought up the children of Israel from the land of Egypt,' but, 'The LORD lives who brought up the children of Israel from the land of the north and from all the lands where He had driven them.' For I will bring them back into their land which I gave to their fathers."* Jeremiah 16:14-15

I remember standing on a kibbutz just outside Jerusalem and meeting a group of Russian Jews a few years ago. Many of them had just arrived from Russia and we were chatting. Eventually one of them asked why I was helping them. I answered that it is because I believe in the God of Abraham, Isaac and Jacob. My answer was quickly interpreted to many languages and a murmur went through the room. After that it was quiet and the presence of God's Spirit came over the room, and some of the immigrants began to cry. "God," some of them whispered over and over again.

**"The Jews, your majesty, the Jews"**
Studying the history of the Jewish people with your Bible open in front of you is a fantastic experience. There is one main theme that runs throughout the course of history, and God's hand is visible in the hardships of the Jewish people. The prophecies that have been pointed out in this book are only a portion of all the prophecies that have foretold real key historical events. One of the most tragic, yet accurate, is Jeremiah's prophecy that when the Jewish people return to Israel they would come "one from a city and two from a family."

## PART IV — THE END TIMES

*"Return, O backsliding children," says the LORD; "for I am married to you. I will take you, one from a city and two from a family, and I will bring you to Zion."* Jeremiah 3:14

Every time I visit Israel I am reminded of this verse. In my conversations with the Jews, this traumatic background is very common, that "she was the only one who survived from that village," or "he is the only one that survived in his family." That is why I no longer ask a Jew about his history, or where he comes from, because it always brings the trauma of the past to mind. Besides, I don't need to ask because I already know that they came "one from a city and two from a family"—the others were exterminated in the Holocaust.

It is said that Frederick the Great of Prussia, who was basically an atheist, once said to his personal physician, who was a very pious man: "Give me proof that there is a God. But speed it up, I'm in a hurry!" to which the doctor quickly replied: "The Jews, your majesty, the Jews." ✡

## Before The Final Battle: The Gospel Will Be Preached And The Jews Will Return Home

**H**ISTORY CAN BE DIVIDED into seven great epochs. Today we are living in the sixth and next to last epoch, the one before eternity enters the scene once again. The last great event, which also initiated the epoch of time in which we live today, was when God became man and walked among us 2,000 years ago. The Bible teaches that he "entered into" the world and that he "went out of" the world. The worldwide transformation that was set into motion then is still going on today. As the church expanded and the Jewish people fled from place to place, a foundation was laid for a new, worldwide culture and body of concepts and values: the Judeo-Christian worldview. In the Jewish system of values there was also an essential core belief in one God—the God of Abraham, Isaac and Jacob. The system of values that our entire western society has been built upon can be traced to the laws, ethics and religious rules that were communicated by God to the Jewish people at Mt. Sinai. Here we discover yet another of the paradoxes of history: the Europe that has been permeated by anti-Semitism throughout the centuries is built upon the system of values established by Judaism!

Those who can interpret the signs of the times understand that the epochs of time are in the process of shifting. Today we know that the ozone layer that protects us from the dangerous rays of the sun has been seriously damaged. The rainforest that produces oxygen and is so vital to maintaining balance in the atmosphere is on the verge of disappearing. Water has become a precious commodity in third world countries. We are in the middle of a population explosion where region after region is over-populated. There is a gigantic cloud of carbon dioxide resting over Asia today that keeps the sun from being able to emerge clearly, and researchers warn about the future consequences of the greenhouse effect, which will raise the temperature of the atmosphere and unleash powers of nature so great that no one can foresee the extent of such catastrophes. There are indications of all this and much more in the prophecies about the end times that reappear throughout the Bible. A distant future is spoken of in which the earth has come to the end of its time, where the development of man has reached its uttermost limit, and where catastrophes of nature and wars are rampant.

So when will the earth come to the end of its time, and when will God's purposes for the world have been fulfilled? I know that everyone who has tried to interpret this in their own time has failed. But there are signs of our current times that indicate that the end is near, that the sixth epoch of time is reaching its culmination, and that huge upheavals are around the corner. But Jesus teaches that no one knows the exact "times and seasons"—except the God of Abraham, Isaac and Jacob.

**The gospel is being preached—The Jews are being forced to move from place to place**
When Jesus rose from the dead and the sixth epoch of time com-

menced, it was the source of two major movements in which we can see how God's plans and purposes unfolded.

The first major movement was that the gospel went forth to all peoples. One thing that the people around Jesus continually asked him about was when he planned to restore David's fallen tent, the kingdom of the Messiah. When would he establish the Messianic world-dominating kingdom, with Jerusalem as its capital city, as foretold by the prophets? (see Is. 2:1–5, Micah 4:1–5, Zech. 9:10, Is. 11, Zech. 14). The Jewish people's concept of the Messiah, the great king, comes from the prophetic books. But in the Old Testament the Messiah is revealed as having two completely separate missions; on the one hand he is the suffering servant who bears and atones for the iniquities of the world with his own life; on the other hand he is the great king who comes to rule the world based out of Jerusalem. The first time the Messiah came it was as the suffering servant, to give his life as a ransom for the world. The next time he will come as the great king. The Jews were, for obvious reasons, focused on the kingly mission and asked many times when the Messianic kingdom would be established on the earth.

When Jesus gave his life on the cross, all Messianic hopes were transformed into despair for a few days. But when Jesus' disciples got to meet the risen Christ, a new hope grew for the immediate establishment of the Messianic kingdom again, and the question was asked anew: "Lord," the disciples asked, "are you at this time going to restore the kingdom to Israel?" Jesus was very clear in his answer. He said: "It is not for you to know times or seasons which the Father has put in His own authority. But you shall receive power when the Holy Spirit has come upon you; and you shall be witnesses to Me in Jerusalem, and in all Judea and Samaria, and to the end of the earth" (Acts 1:6–8). In another passage Jesus says: "And this gospel of the kingdom will be preached in all the world as a witness to all the nations, and then the end will come" (Matt 24:14). We who are alive at this period in history can see that things really did turn out this way. Even though the enormous expansion that got underway during those first 300 years has slowed down, the message of the kingdom of God has continued to expand so that it has reached nearly all people groups today. Actually, the revival church that exploded in the beginning of the 1900s (the Pentecostal movement) is the world's fastest growing movement ever by far: from zero to about 550 million in 100 years!

The second major movement was when Jews all over the world began their nearly 2,000-year-long walk down the Via Dolorosa. In the Bible it is mentioned many times that the Jewish people are God's witnesses. In each country where the Jews arrived, they were a testimony. Even if the Jews didn't "evangelize" and actively seek to win people over to their faith, their lives and obedience to the Law of Moses was a sign that pointed beyond the law to the one and only God. The book of Revelation speaks of martyrs. We Christians have underlined those verses, but how many Jews have suffered the death of a martyr? How many Jews have been killed because they refused to deny their faith in the covenant that was made at Mt. Sinai? Can you think of the Jews without thinking of God? Probably not, since their entire life history testifies to the one and only God!

**Things are coming full circle**
Today we can see that the two major movements that were started 2,000 years ago at the beginning of the sixth epoch of time are completing their courses. The Jews reached the four corners of the earth in the middle of the 1800s, and are now on their way back to Israel. Even the first movement is being completed. We are starting to see an end in sight to the task Jesus gave the apostles: to preach the gospel to all people groups. In most countries and groups of people there are living churches today, with active, committed members.

It is wonderful to observe that a true brotherhood has emerged between parts of the church and the Jewish people. It all seems to fall perfectly into place within God's plan. As the Jews reached the four corners of the earth, the revival church also exploded around the same time. Bible verses that have been obscured and wrapped in lies because of strong anti-Semitic vibes in the church are now seen in the correct light. The result is that pastors and believers see the Jewish people from the perspective of the Bible.

## With the sons of Israel in your arms and her daughters on your shoulders

> *He will set up a banner for the nations, and will assemble the outcasts of Israel, and gather together the dispersed of Judah from the four corners of the earth.* Isaiah 11:12

The banner that was set up is Jesus, and in the 1800s parts of the church began to re-evaluate the traditional view of the Jews. The new revival movements that erupted in western Europe and the USA were quick to discover the lies of anti-Semitism. The revival church was established in place after place and as that happened, Christians began to actively work to help and bless the Jewish people. Preachers and pastors started to teach that the Jews are God's chosen people and possession, and during the 1900s this doctrine gained a lot of ground. There might not have been very many who thought this way at first, but as the revival church has gradually conquered the world, these attitudes have spread. It is a crucial step to go from recognizing the task of the Jews in God's plan of salvation history to then actively helping Jews come home to Israel, and for many people that step is a big one. Think about this: in the beginning of the Bible, in Genesis 12, God says that he who blesses Abraham's descendants will be blessed. Doing good toward the Jewish people, all according to the covenant between Abraham and God, is the same as doing good toward God himself! Besides that, the Bible contains clear teaching that indicates that we should actively help the Jewish people return to Israel.

> *Thus says the Lord GOD: "Behold, I will lift My hand in an oath to the nations, and set up My standard for the peoples; they shall*

*bring your sons in their arms, and your daughters shall be carried on their shoulders."* Isaiah 49:22

Many Christians become activated when they hear me preach on this verse. It doesn't matter if it is in Sweden, India, Africa or Eastern Europe—even if they have never heard this kind of teaching before, their hearts open up and they understand and are moved by the truth. They know that the banner is Jesus and many get involved, wanting desperately to be enable the final exodus* of the Jewish people, to "come with the sons of Israel in their arms and their daughters on their shoulders." All over the world there are Christians today who acquire a special love for the Jews and who see the big picture and the Lord's holiness in the miracles that are occurring and have occurred in Israel.

In another context, also from the prophet Isaiah, there is another very special association between the return of the Jews and the salvation of the Gentile nations:

*"For I know their works and their thoughts. It shall be that I will gather all nations and tongues; and they shall come and see My glory. I will set a sign among them; and those among them who escape I will send to the nations: to Tarshish and Pul and Lud, who draw the bow, and Tubal and Javan, to the coastlands afar off who have not heard My fame nor seen My glory. And they shall declare My glory among the Gentiles. Then they shall bring all your brethren for an offering to the LORD out of all nations, on horses and in chariots and in litters, on mules and on camels, to My holy mountain Jerusalem," says the LORD, "as the children of Israel bring an offering in a clean vessel into the house of the LORD. And I will also take some of them for priests and Levites," says the LORD.* Isaiah 66:18–21

"There will come a time," Isaiah foresees, "when the Gentile peoples will see the glory of the Lord." The glory of the Lord is Jesus;

he is the glorified one, in him is reflected God's perfect glory. The Gentiles, who live in the "distance," will receive "a sign." The sign is the child of the virgin, Jesus. The Lord will "gather" these Gentiles. When they gather together they will be the church of his glory. Some from this church will be sent as "messengers" (Greek Apóstolos) to the Gentiles "who have not heard" about God, or seen his "glory"— Jesus. In the future these Gentile peoples will, as a token of thanks to God that they were brought into his glory, and because they follow and obey Jesus, bring the Jewish people out of the Gentile nations, home to Israel and to God's holy mountain in Jerusalem!

> *"When I have brought them back from the peoples and gathered them out of their enemies' lands, and I am hallowed in them in the sight of many nations, then they shall know that I am the LORD their God, who sent them into captivity among the nations, but also brought them back to their land, and left none of them captive any longer. And I will not hide My face from them anymore; for I shall have poured out My Spirit on the house of Israel," says the Lord GOD.* Ezekiel 39: 27–29

When this time comes, and we are at that point right now, the return of the Jewish people to Israel will speak with prophetic accuracy and encouragement to many Gentile Christian churches and individual believers. Their return will be more than a re-immigration. Their return will be a sign of God's power and an indication of where we find ourselves on God's prophetic clock. This in its turn will cause more Christians to get involved with the work to bring the Jewish people home to Israel and to God's holy mountain in Jerusalem. "And," Ezekiel prophesies, "not one will be left behind."

## The spiritual essence of the church is reflected in the history of the Jewish people

The innermost motive of the church is tested and revealed in the history of the Jewish people. There is a church that has persecuted the

Jews and indirectly been responsible for much of the sufferings and deaths of the Jews for 2,000 years. But there is another church at the opposite end of that spectrum. Compelled by self-sacrificing love, it fights for Israel and for the Jewish people. ✡

## The Final Battle

**B**EFORE THE CULMINATION of world history into the seventh and final epoch of time—the Messianic epoch—world opinion will turn yet again against the Jewish people. I don't personally like the thought of this, but a final power struggle is predestined to happen, and the way it will all play out is hard to predict. The fact that it will happen is unavoidable. Based on the light the prophets of the Bible cast over the end times, all of these things will occur as a result of "the full number of the Gentiles having come in." In Paul's letter to the Romans he quotes Isaiah when he foresees, as he puts it, "this mystery":

> *For I do not desire, brethren, that you should be ignorant of this mystery, lest you should be wise in your own opinion, that blindness in part has happened to Israel until the fullness of the Gentiles has come in. And so all Israel will be saved, as it is written:*

> *"The Deliverer will come out of Zion, and He will turn away ungodliness from Jacob; for this is My covenant with them, when I take away their sins."* Concerning the gospel they are enemies for your sake, but concerning the election they are beloved for the sake of the fathers. For the gifts and the calling of God are irrevocable. Romans 11:25–29, compare Isaiah 27:9 and 59:20

So there is a set number of people, a "full" number of Gentiles who are going to come into God's kingdom. This "time of mercy" is still ongoing, and that "mercy" is the very consequence of the age in which we now live, that a certain number of Gentiles will be "grafted" into the true olive tree, Israel (see Romans 11). When Jesus taught the disciples about the last days he talked about the same scenario: "Jerusalem will be trampled by Gentiles until the times of the Gentiles are fulfilled" (Luke 21:24). One day in the future this "time of the Gentiles" will be complete. So it is clearly shown in this Bible verse that there will be a point at which the Gentiles will no longer have the possibility of turning to God, since the blessing God promised through Abraham's seed (see Gen. 12:1–3) has reached all peoples. When all of these things occur, all of Jerusalem will be set free. You could say that time is working in favor of the Jewish people, but that time is running out for the Gentiles.

## Jerusalem's third temple

> *… so that he sits as God in the temple of God, showing himself that he is God.* 2 Thessalonians 2:4, compare Daniel 11:36

Many people who study the Biblical prophecies are asking themselves if it is fair to believe that a third temple will be built. Islam reigns on the temple mount in Jerusalem and the Dome of the Rock mosque is now located where the Jewish temple was once said to be located. But the temple wasn't actually located there!

Ancient accounts of history tell of the straight line that was formed from the Mount of Olives in through King Solomon's gate to the holiest of holies, which was the very center of the temple. But that is not where the Dome of the Rock is located! There is—and this is remarkable—an area on the temple mount that has not been built upon, and this space is the exact spot where the temple itself stood.

There is a movement in Jerusalem today called "The Temple Institute." They are preparing for the inauguration of the third temple. They have flags, horns, and the robes of the high priest ready to be used, but are waiting for a few remaining details before they are able to reinstate the high priest into his office.

Another twist to all of this is that there has been talk of building a Jewish temple, a synagogue, on the temple site.

This was brought up in the Camp David discussions that preceded the intifada that broke out in 2001. A logical political solution to the Jerusalem issue and a possible future scenario is that the temple mount and Jerusalem will be the capital city for all religions and, as a point of negotiation, the Jews will even be offered a part of the temple mount where the former temple stood!

## A new world leader will emerge on the stage of history

> ... that Day will not come unless the falling away comes first, and the man of sin is revealed, the son of perdition, who opposes and exalts himself above all that is called God or that is worshiped ... according to the working of Satan, with all power, signs, and lying wonders, and with all unrighteous deception among those who perish. 2 Thessalonians 2:3-4, 9-10, compare Daniel 11:36

In the future, as history approaches its climax, a new world leader will come forth. This will be a charismatic person who has a worldwide political plan of action that he claims will fix the big problems that are threatening all of mankind. His political stance will be both democratic and totalitarian at the same time; all objective values must be forsaken so that everything and everyone can be accepted.

The political message will be: "It is only natural that all exclusivity has to cease, so everything will melt into one single international fellowship." Under this doctrine a subjective society will develop where no objective values will be allowed to have any say, since the foundation of this new political stance is that everyone has to accept everyone else. In this society the teaching of the Bible will be seen as a threat since it claims objective truths about one God and one way to God. It speaks of values that cannot be compromised; it speaks about what is right and wrong.

In the religious syncretism that the politics of this "new age" represent, there is no room for religious exclusivity. You will no longer be able to claim that the God of the Bible is the only God and that all other religions are wrong! This reasoning will have the appearance of being completely logical and rational. The mantra of this new world religion will be: "How can we have peace in the world if one religion thinks that it is better than all others? We all have a part in what is divine and all religions worship the same god." It will be one world religion that, while recognizing all religions, simultaneously disapproves of all of them.

In this situation two conservative movements will be persecuted more than any others. One will be the true Christian church, whose members will risk their lives to firmly maintain that there is only one God and that the way to him can only be found through Jesus. The second movement is the Jewish people. If they haven't let go of their Jewish identity, their historical roots or the system of values they received from God at the foot of Mt. Sinai nearly 3,500 years ago, why would they give up their exclusivity now?

## Jerusalem—a cup of drunkenness to all the surrounding peoples

> *"I will make Jerusalem a cup of drunkenness to all the surrounding peoples, when they lay siege against Judah and Jerusalem. And it shall happen in that day that I will make Jerusalem a very heavy stone for all peoples; all who would heave it away*

*will surely be cut in pieces, though all nations of the earth are gathered against it."* Zechariah 12:2–3

As a result of the Jewish people's stubborn resistance to being absorbed by the rest of the world, the dark scenario of anti-Semitism will once again play itself out. The powers that worked through Pharaoh, Haman and Hitler will be incarnated in the leading politicians of the end times. Anti-Semitism will grow, and this time it will be total and worldwide. The Jews will, as they always have, claim Jerusalem as their city, and they will point to the promises in the Bible and claim their exclusivity in God. In the future all political negotiations concerning Jerusalem will collapse. In the new world order, Jerusalem's status as the capital city of all religions will make up the cornerstone for world politics and it may even be established as the capital city of the world. All peoples will want to own Jerusalem and will be intoxicated by the drawing power the city seems to have. The problem is the Jews. As they always have, "through water and fire," they will stubbornly refuse to give up their exclusive right to Jerusalem.

**The next item on the political agenda**
The political solution will be to force a solution to the "Jewish problem" by military means. This is a future development that is absolutely not just an eschatological theory but rather, as I judge it, something very real based on sensible political assessment. There are already many different international military actions that are organized against regimes that have been assessed as threats to world peace or strong political interests. The possibility of making Jerusalem an international protectorate that is governed by the United Nations is already being addressed. But world opinion is not quite ready for that yet. However, when Muslim and Asian dictatorships are tamed and neutralized, the issue of Jerusalem will come up and the religious tensions there will be the next item on the agenda for a new world order. But what will happen is that the people who have always chosen martyrdom before giving up their exclusivity will

make the same choice yet again. *I will pour out the spirit of grace and supplication; then they will look on me whom they pierced.*

When Jesus wept on the Mount of Olives and looked into the future he said: "You shall see Me no more till you say, 'Blessed is He who comes in the name of the LORD'" (Matt. 23:39, compare Ps. 118:26). Christians have always made a claim on this prophecy, but it was spoken over the Jewish people. Concerning the political crisis that will erupt and result in the attack of Israel once again by foreign armies, Zechariah foresaw a fantastic intervention by God:

> *It shall be in that day that I will seek to destroy all the nations that come against Jerusalem. And I will pour on the house of David and on the inhabitants of Jerusalem the Spirit of grace and supplication; then they will look on Me whom they pierced. Yes, they will mourn for Him as one mourns for his only son, and grieve for Him as one grieves for a firstborn. In that day there shall be a great mourning in Jerusalem, like the mourning at Hadad Rimmon in the plain of Megiddo. And the land shall mourn, every family by itself: the family of the house of David by itself, and their wives by themselves; the family of the house of Nathan by itself, and their wives by themselves; the family of the house of Levi by itself, and their wives by themselves; the family of Shimei by itself, and their wives by themselves; all the families that remain, every family by itself, and their wives by themselves. In that day a fountain shall be opened for the house of David and for the inhabitants of Jerusalem, for sin and for uncleanness.* Zechariah 12:9–13:1

Concerning the political and military chaos that is going to characterize Israel, and the resulting deaths of many, the prophet Zechariah writes:

> *… two-thirds in it shall be cut off and die, but one-third shall be left in it: I will bring the one-third through the fire, will refine*

*them as silver is refined, and test them as gold is tested. They will call on My name, and I will answer them. I will say, "This is My people"; and each one will say, "The LORD is my God."* Zechariah 13:8–9

Eventually there will only be one way out: to cry out to God in the same way their ancestors have done so many times. But not just to God, but now even to the Messiah, since things will have come to the point that the anti-Semitic spirit of murder will be burning across the earth and the only thing that can save the Jewish people is for the Messiah to break into the realm of time. During this time of revelation, brokenness, prayer and cries to the God of the covenant for the promises of the Messiah to be fulfilled, Zechariah's prophecies will be fulfilled. As war rages all around and gets closer and closer, a spiritual awakening will occur in large portions of the Jewish people. The "spirit of grace and supplication" that is then poured out over Israel will fill the people with an inner longing for God! The synagogues will be filled to capacity on the Sabbath and people everywhere will talk about the Messiah.

The fact that the synagogues are filled and that the Jews, instead of giving up their religious exclusivity, seem to intensify their faith in God even more, will be broadcast to every home across the world. Once again, one last time, the Jews will be a testimony to the one and only God and Messiah. In this spiritual awakening Jesus will be revealed to the Jewish people. In their inner man they will sense his nearness on a spiritual level and they will see that the Messiah and the Jesus whom the Romans crucified 2,000 years ago are one and the same person. New light will be cast over the prophecies in the Bible and everything will be revealed to all who believe in the God of Abraham, Isaac and Jacob.

## The final battle
Three times before, political world leaders have tried to exterminate the Jewish people, but each time God has raised up a savior, a leader

who has confronted the anti-Semitic leader and saved the people at the last minute. The first time was in Egypt, the second time in Babylon and the third time in Germany. It was Moses against Pharaoh, Esther against the Agagite Haman and in one way you could say Herzl against Hitler. It is interesting to see the associations between the attempts at extermination and the land of Israel. Each attempt at extermination occurred in connection with the Jews heading back to their land. Why? Because the Jewish people have a dual task in the history of salvation. The first was to birth the Messiah, which occurred in Bethlehem 2,000 years ago. The second is to receive the Messiah when he once again enters the world. This is the task that both the land and the people have! This was at the core of the covenant: "In your descendants," God promised, "the whole world will be blessed." Here we see yet another paradox: the Jewish people who were blamed for being murderers and conspirators against humanity are actually the exact opposite. They are the salvation of the Gentiles since they birthed the Messiah, and they are the future of the world since they have been chosen to receive the Messiah when he returns once again.

The question everyone should ask themselves is: which powers have been at work behind anti-Semitism? What fruit have these powers borne? What would the world look like today if we had continued to build upon the pagan religions with their warrior cultures and slave societies? If Jewish ethics, morals and values had not broken through when the Jew Jesus taught and preached, would we still have had witch-burnings at the stake in Scandinavia, would we have exalted emperors as gods and found predictions in the stars?

When the time has come for the Messiah to come into the world, the final battle will be between the forces that have done so much damage to so many people and the Power that is the source of all things and the future salvation of all things!

## The final attempt at extermination

One final time, hatred will mount against the Jewish people. This

## The Final Battle

time it will be more serious than ever. The leader who will act will do so with all of the gathered powers of darkness in one and the same person. It is the fullness of the beast who mercilessly makes a final desperate attempt to annihilate the people who, throughout all of their history, have refused to worship him and have always claimed that there is only one God. It is Satan himself who will make the final attempt to hinder the fulfillment of the ancient prophecies, those that say that the Messiah will break in and that a world order will be established in which love and truth are complete.

In that hour, when the false game of evil seems to have deceived the world and the solution to the "Jewish problem" once and for all seems to have reached its full conclusion, history will take a new turn one last time. The whole world will closely follow the Jews' stubborn battle against the gathered international force that is sent against the Jewish people in Israel in order to set Jerusalem free in the name of peace. "You will see Me no more," Jesus said to his beloved people, "till you say 'Blessed is He who comes in the name of the Lord.'" On screens all over the world there will be reports of battles and of the world's gathered troops standing on the hills outside of Jerusalem. When the final battle begins, synagogues all across the world will be filled with Jews. They know that now only one thing can save them, and that is the Messiah. Everywhere prayers about the coming of the Messiah will be heard, "Blessed is He who comes in the name of the Lord."

Then it will happen. When the beast's fury is at its peak, when the leaders of the world are most intoxicated with lust for Jerusalem, and when the anti-Semitic spirit of murder burns the strongest, God will raise up his final leader and savior. This time it won't be Moses, or Queen Esther, or the journalist Herzl. Now the time and hour will have come when the earth is ripe. Across the whole world people will comprehend it, a deafening thunder that breaks forth into the realm of time—the sound of a bassoon that everyone can hear, the powers of the skies are shaken and the signs of the Son of Man will be visible to all. In Jerusalem everything will culminate when the Messiah breaks into our dimension. Everyone will be able to see him when he breaks through the skies and plants his feet on the mount east of Jerusalem, on the Mount of Olives (see Matt. 24:29–31 and Is. 13:10).

> *For I will gather all the nations to battle against Jerusalem ... Then the LORD will go forth and fight against those nations, as He fights in the day of battle. And in that day His feet will stand on the Mount of Olives, which faces Jerusalem on the east ... Thus the LORD my God will come, and all the saints with You ... and the LORD shall be King over all the earth.* Zechariah 14:2–5, 9

The Jewish people's task in the history of salvation will be complete. They birthed the Messiah, they "went through water and fire" and showed themselves to be "worthy" covenant partners with the living God. They held out against everything and everyone and finally got to meet the Messiah they had waited for for so long.

Now creation goes into its final epoch, the Sabbath rest, and in this thousand-year reign the Jewish people will be at the center of the worldwide kingdom of peace that will be based out of the Jews' capital city of Jerusalem.

> *Now it shall come to pass in the latter days that the mountain of the LORD's house shall be established on the top of the mountains, and shall be exalted above the hills; and all nations shall flow to it. Many people shall come and say, "Come, and let us go up to the mountain of the LORD, to the house of the God of Jacob; He will teach us His ways, and we shall walk in His paths." For out of Zion shall go forth the law, and the word of the LORD from Jerusalem. He shall judge between the nations, and rebuke many people; they shall beat their swords into plowshares, and their spears into pruning hooks; nation shall not lift up sword against nation, neither shall they learn war anymore.* Isaiah 2:2–4 ✡

# EPILOGUE

**N**OW SOMEONE MIGHT SAY: "But then the Jews will realize that we Christians have been right all along." My friend, the Jews were never wrong! Everything that has happened to them has happened for our sake! Everything has been a part of God's plan to save mankind. The Jews were not wrong when they held on to the covenant with Abraham, when they refused to forsake the Law of Moses, or when they stubbornly held on to their Jewish identity. What about the new covenant in Jesus? The new covenant in Christ rests on the old covenant, and it would have been impossible to make the new one a reality if it hadn't been preceded by the old one. Both of the covenants actually have the overall purpose of saving mankind from destruction. The Jews' responsibility was to enter into the first covenant and thereby be the ones who paved the way for the new covenant, a covenant that will result in eternal life for all people.

God's plan of salvation included a period of time when a portion of the Jews would not be able to see that Jesus is their Messiah. God determined that this would happen (compare Rom. 11:25–26). It is during this period (which is still going on) that the gospel of God's kingdom is being preached to all the Gentiles. I don't know why, but the Bible teaches that during this period of time when the Gentiles can enter God's kingdom, the majority of the Jewish people will not be able to discover that Jesus is the Messiah. The reason for this, according to the Bible, is not because they are rejected by God, but rather it is for our sake, so that the Gentiles can be saved (compare Rom. 11:11b).

However, the Gentiles will be judged according to their response to the gospel, since during the age of the Gentiles, the sixth epoch, every Gentile who hears the gospel can make their own choice about whether or not to receive the salvation that God has prepared for us. When the veil is lifted and everything is revealed to everyone, when we see what is hidden today and clearly understand the mystery of the universe, then everyone—most of all we Christians—will realize how wrong we have been about the Jews and how wrongly we have treated the Jewish people throughout history. We will discover that the blessing we have received has its origins in the covenant that God made with the Jews. We will understand that the Jewish people have been persecuted because of the truth and because of the wonderful tasks they were entrusted with. The first was to birth God into the world; the second will be to receive him when he comes back. Many who call themselves Christians will be devastated when they realize that they cut off the way to their own salvation when they accused the Jews of killing Christ. After all, there is only one basis for salvation: believing that God became man to freely give his life as a ransom for fallen mankind.

In eternity you and I will commend our Jewish brothers and sisters for so stubbornly holding on to the covenant. For refusing to give up their identity despite all the anti-Semitic persecution. For holding on to Israel and for standing firm in Jerusalem as a chosen group of people at the end of time, alone against the whole world and crying out to the Messiah until he—when the time was right—again broke into our world and established the true kingdom, the Messianic kingdom of peace. After having been the most ridiculed people in all of history, the Jewish people will truly be seen as the heroes of eternity! ✡

# Tommy Lilja ministries

## *What we are doing is for real!*

What we are doing is for real – and it's the fruit of what many people do together. That is why you are important. Only you can be the real difference, only you can do what you were meant to do in this life. In my ministry I have the opportunity to work with many wonderful people like you. I count it as a gift from God, something I greatly value.

When we partner together with you, it enables us to carry out the command and will of Jesus. This has resulted in a dynamic partnership, a collaboration whose fruit depends on what many people are doing together, and that fruit has been extensive. This is what we do:

### *Reach – Every Time, All the Time and Everywhere*

From the third world to nations like Sweden and the United States, our goal is the same: to reach as many people as possible. Why? Because what we are doing is for real. Reaching people with the gospel is the ultimate purpose of what we do - and it doesn't get any more real than that.

- *Saving, healing, delivering and restoring people.*
- *Evangelization crusades among the unreached peoples and in inaccessible places.*
- *Different kinds of Bible schools, leadership seminars and developmental aid.*
- *Church planting that has resulted in reaching unreached people groups.*
- *Global TV to help us reach beyond the walls.*

My TV program is called "Watch and Believe." Its purpose is to show what Jesus is doing in the world today. Seen in many countries and in many languages, its reach is extensive. When viewers watch the reality of what Jesus is doing today, we are helping them believe.

### Return and Restore – Bring my People Home

Did you know that the Scripture speaks of a second exodus, just as great as when Moses led Israel out of Egypt? That exodus is taking place today, and with our project Operation Great Exodus we are a part of the action. What we are doing is for real.

- *We have helped over 20,000 Jews from all over the world return home to Israel, and we continue to help about 1,000 Jews home each year.*
- *In Israel we are an active part of helping the newcomers and giving shelter to hurting children.*

### Refuge – A Shelter for Children in Need

We enable orphaned street children, many with HIV, to encounter Jesus and receive a stable and safe upbringing. What we are doing is for real. The reality is that there are children living alone on the street, and our goal is to give them refuge.

In Tommy Lilja Ministries we have committed ourselves to doing the work of God and we welcome you to become a part of that work. What we are doing is for real. The more of us who work together, the more we can get done, and above all: only you can do what you are meant to do. That is why you are important, whoever you are, we welcome you to become a part of what we are doing – it's for real, and we will accomplish it together.

*In Christ,*
*yours sincerely,*
*Tommy Lilja*

**2004, Jerusalem.** *Tommy in a meeting with Israeli minister Naomi Blumenthal. Since the end of the nineties, when Operation Great Exodus really took off, Pastor Tommy has had an open door to top Israeli officials, resulting in many meetings with ministers and prime ministers in Israel. The gratitude they express toward Tommy and all the supporters of Operation Great Exodus is overwhelming. It is very special to the Jews that they have friends outside of Israel.*

**2003, Jerusalem.** *Tommy in a meeting with Israel's former deputy prime minister Natan Sharansky. Minister Sharansky, a legend in his own lifetime, spent many years in a Soviet prison for allegedly spying for Israel. Sharansky has personally expressed his appreciation for Tommy's book* **"The Jews - Heroes of Eternity."**

**2005, Stockholm, Sweden.** *Ceremony of gratitude from the Ambassador of Israel to Tommy and Carina, and to everyone who has supported Operation Great Exodus. The ambassador is handing over a piece of art to Tommy for having helped 5,000 Jews back home to Israel by 2005.*

**2006, Stockholm, Sweden.** *Another meeting with Israel's ambassador, Benny Dagan. Since the start of Operation Great Exodus, Tommy has been in close contact with top officials from Israel.*

**Ben Gurion Airport, Tel Aviv.** *Since it started in 1996, Operation Great Exodus has helped more than 20,000 Jews back home to Israel. It has been an exciting journey, filled with obstacles but mostly blessings.*

**Ben Gurion Airport, Tel Aviv.** *In 2009, Tommy and Carina were granted special permission from Israeli Airport Security, one of the most restrictive in the world, to be on the tarmac to welcome the flight that brought the 10,000th Jew to Israel.*

**Ben Gurion Airport, Tel Aviv.** *In this photo from 2009, Tommy and Carina are accepting a certificate from Jewish officials confirming that they have helped 10,000 Jews return to Israel. By 2014 that number had reached 20,000.*

**Neve Michael Children's Home.** *Since its start in 1996, Operation Great Exodus, a branch of Tommy Lilja Ministries, has helped more than 20,000 Jews back home to Israel. But that's just the beginning. They have also been involved in several social projects within Israel, including providing economic support to nursing homes for Holocaust survivors and supporting children's homes like Neve Michael.*

**2010, Tel Aviv, Israel.** *Tommy and Carina greet a returning Jewish family from Ethiopia. Tommy's organization Operation Great Exodus has helped Jews from all around the world back home to Israel, from the lost tribe of Manasseh (northeastern India) to the lost tribe of Dan (Ethiopia).*

**2011, Jerusalem.** *Tommy and Carina are visiting one of the absorption centers in Israel, where immigrants come and receive help to assimilate into their new country. Here they are sitting with some children in kindergarten.*

**2013, Jerusalem.** *Tommy in a conversation with Rabbi Ariel and Rabbi Jafet on the hills of Jerusalem. On this day in 2013, 25,000 of the returning Ethiopian Jews had gathered and Tommy was there to participate. It was from this spot that God showed Abraham Mt. Moriah, the place where he was to sacrifice his son Isaac.*

# Tommy Lilja
ministries

Tommy and Carina Lilja are impacting the entire globe with the love of Jesus Christ. Their extensive organization includes church plants, Bible schools, leadership training, evangelistic crusades, children's centers, TV programs and book publishing. In addition, Tommy Lilja Ministries helps thousands of Jews home to Israel every year.

For More Information About Tommy Lilja Ministries,
Visit www.TommyLilja.org